America's Most Wanted Recipes

Volume 2

Ron Douglas

The Secret Recipes for Your Favorite Dishes

LEGAL STATEMENT

Recipe Secrets.net and Verity Associates, LLC are not sponsored, endorsed, or affiliated with any recipe source. We disclaim using any copyright or trademark.

This document is a compilation of recipes and cooking tips based on personal interpretation of the foods listed. Through trial and error, each recipe was created to taste the same as, or similar to, its restaurant/brand counterpart, but they are not the actual recipes used by the manufacturer or creator.

The brand or restaurant names for the recipes have only been included as an aid in cataloging the recipes and do not imply authenticity or endorsement by the manufacturer or creator. All restaurant and company names are trademarks of their respective owners. Please see our Trademarks section towards the end of this cookbook for detailed trademark credits.

All information provided through this cookbook is intended to be accurate. However, there may be inaccuracies at times which we will make every attempt to correct when found. Some of the information provided may be intended to assist you in making decisions but does not eliminate the need to discuss your particular circumstances with a qualified professional.

For the actual and authentic version of the food products listed in this compilation, please patronize the individual restaurant or manufacturer.

To the best of the author's knowledge, all company related information and trademark details are true and accurate. Any misrepresentation of factual material is unintentional.

ISBN: 978-1-59872-941-2

Printed in the United States of America

Published and distributed by: Verity Associates, LLC - PO Box 670361
Kew Gardens Hills, NY 11367

To my dear friends from The Secret Recipe Forum,

thanks for your contributions and continued support.

www.RecipeSecrets.net/forum

PREFACE

After the huge success of Volume 1, due to popular demand, we're back again with *America's Most Wanted Recipes Volume 2.*

With the help of the 45,000 members of our Secret Recipe Forum, we've tested, replicated, and compiled the recipes for 101 of the most beloved restaurant dishes in America. These are the "secret recipes" which are generating billions of dollars for the restaurant industry every year. Now you can have them to prepare in your own kitchen!

I can go on and on about how accurate these clone recipes are but I think one of our customers explains it best:

> "I have made MANY of the recipes, and have been thrilled EVERY time, so have all the friends and family that I have cooked for. Everybody who gets to taste my cooking says how amazing it is that these recipes taste just like the restaurants.
>
> I was in the restaurant field for close to 4 years, and I know that everything is premade, boxed, bagged, and full of blubber ready to be assembled. I love that I get the same great flavor, with out the excess fat and preservatives. It's healthy, full of flavor, and I already have all of the ingredients in my kitchen.
>
> I shock myself every time I cook! I keep on wanting to compliment the cook, and then I remember that I am the cook.
>
> Thanks for helping me to realize that I love cooking!"
>
> --Martina M.

We encourage you to put the book to good use and make these famous dishes yourself. Once you've tried the recipes, you'll see what makes them so special and why we have so many satisfied customers.

You can also get thousands of additional recipes and interact with our online community through our Secret Recipe Forum. To sign up for free go to: www.RecipeSecrets.net/forum

I hope this cookbook brings enjoyment for you, your family and friends for years to come.

Ron Douglas
Author of *America's Most Wanted Recipes: Volumes 1 & 2*

CONTENTS

*Applebee's Chicken Quesadilla Grande

Ingredients

1/2 ounce shortening
2 (12-inch) flour tortillas
2 tablespoon chipotle sauce
4 ounces grilled chicken, warm
1 cup shredded lettuce
Sour cream
Green onion
Salsa

Quesa Filling (use as desired)

Jack and Cheddar cheeses
Jalapeno pepper, diced
Tomato, diced
Onion, diced
Cilantro, minced
Bacon, fried and crumbled

1. Brush one side of each tortilla with shortening.

2. Place one tortilla, shortening side down on work surface. Spread chipotle sauce out on one tortilla.

3. Spread out chicken evenly on top of the sauce on tortilla.

4. Evenly spread Quesa Filling over the chicken. Cover with the other tortilla, shortening side up.

5. Brown on a non stick pan evenly on both sides until internal filling is heated thoroughly.

6. Serve with lettuce, sour cream, green onion and salsa as accompaniments. Add crumbled bacon on top (optional).

RecipeSecrets.net tip:
Serve with Spanish rice, guacamole, and salsa.

Serves 1

*Applebee's Crispy Orange Chicken Skillet

Ingredients

2 pounds boneless, skinless chicken
1 egg
1 1/2 teaspoons salt
1/4 teaspoon pepper
1 tablespoon vegetable oil
1/2 cup plus 1 tablespoon cornstarch
oil (for frying)

Glaze:
1 teaspoon minced garlic
1 1/2 teaspoons grated orange rind
1 cup fresh orange juice
1/2 cup hoisin sauce
Dash cayenne pepper
1/4 cup granulated sugar
Salt and pepper to taste

1. Cut chicken into 2-inch pieces and place in a large bowl. Add in egg, salt, pepper and oil. Mix well and set aside.

2. Stir cornstarch and flour together in another large bowl until mixed well. Add chicken to the flour mixture, and coat each piece well.

3. Pour about a 1/2-inch of oil in a heavy skillet and set over high heat. When the temperature reaches 375 degrees F, carefully add chicken pieces in small batches and fry 3 to 4 minutes or until brown and crunchy.

4. Carefully remove chicken from oil with slotted spoon and drain on paper towels. Continue frying chicken until all are nicely browned and crisp. Set aside and begin to make the glaze.

5. Allow the oil in the skillet to cool slightly, then remove all but 2 tablespoons of oil and put over medium heat. Saute garlic in oil for 1 minute, do not burn.

6. Add remaining ingredients and bring to a boil. While stirring, boil for 3 minutes. Reduce heat and simmer until sauce thickens. Pour glaze over chicken and serve.

Serves 4

*Applebee's Garlic Mashed Potatoes

Ingredients

32 ounces red potatoes
1/2 cup milk
1/4 cup heavy cream
3 tablespoons butter
salt and black pepper, to taste
1/4 cup garlic cloves

1. Place a single layer of garlic cloves on a sheet of aluminum foil and wrap tightly.
2. Roast in 400 degrees F preheated oven for about 45 minutes or until soft.
3. Unwrap and let cool.
4. Peel cloves and set aside until the potatoes are ready.
5. Wash and rinse potatoes under cold water.
6. In large pot, bring red potatoes to a slow boil for about 20 minutes.
7. Remove from heat and drain in colander.
8. In pan or bowl, combine potatoes, peeled and roasted garlic cloves, and all other ingredients and mash with a potato masher.
9. Serve warm.

Serves 8

*Applebee's Low-Fat Grilled Tilapia with Mango Salsa

Ingredients

I Tilapia Fillet (or other whitefish) grilled
1/8 teaspoon cayenne pepper
salt & pepper, to taste
Mango Salsa
White rice
Vegetable Medley

Mango Salsa
I cup diced tomatoes
1/2 cup diced red onions
1/2 each diced jalapeno
2 tablespoon chopped cilantro
Salt and pepper to taste
I teaspoon salad oil
I teaspoon white vinegar
1/2 teaspoon granulated garlic
1/2 cup chopped mango

1. Spray both sides of the tilapia with oil.
2. Shake seasoning (salt, pepper, cayenne pepper) over both sides of the tilapia.
3. Cook tilapia on a clean, lightly oiled grill, smooth side down. Cook to an internal temperature of 145 degrees F, turning once during cooking.
4. Cook rice according to package directions and steam fresh vegetable medley, season with lemon pepper.

Mango Salsa

1. Mix all ingredients but the mango together in a bowl.
2. Add the mango and mix lightly right before serving.

Serves 1

*Applebee's Tomato Basil Soup

Ingredients

5 large Beefsteak tomatoes, peeled, seeded and diced
5 cups V-8 juice
¼ cup onion finely minced
2 garlic cloves; crushed
14 – 18 fresh basil leaves
½ tsp Italian seasoning
1 ¼ cup heavy cream
½ cup butter

salt and pepper to taste
croutons for garnish

1. Place tomatoes and juice in a stock pot over medium heat; simmer for 30 minutes.

2. Add the basil leaves, onions, garlic and Italian seasoning, then puree the tomato mixture with a hand blender.

3. Place in Slow Cooker on low heat.

4. Slowly add the heavy cream and then butter. Season with salt and pepper, to taste.

5. Simmer on low for 1 1/2 to 2 hours. Do not let boil

Serves 6

*Applebee's Walnut Blondie With Maple Butter Sauce

Blondes really do have more fun! This blondie is baked with nuts, topped with both ice cream and chopped walnuts, and served warm covered with a rich, sizzling maple butter sauce.

Ingredients

1/2 teaspoon baking powder
1/8 teaspoon baking soda
1/8 teaspoon salt
1 cup flour, sifted
1/4 cup chopped walnuts (or more)
1/3 cup butter or margarine (melted)
1 cup packed brown sugar
1 egg, beaten
1 tablespoon vanilla extract
1/2 cup white chocolate chips

Maple Butter Sauce:

3/4 cup maple syrup
1/2 cup butter
3/4 cup brown sugar
1/4 cup chopped walnuts (optional)

RecipeSecrets.net tip:

For the best flavor, use REAL maple syrup in this recipe.

1. Preheat the oven to 350 degrees F.

2. Add baking powder, baking soda and salt to the already sifted flour. Next, sift dry ingredients again. Add chopped nuts and mix well. Set aside.

3. Add brown sugar to melted butter and mix well. Then mix in egg and vanilla extract.

4. Add flour mixture, a little at a time, until mixed well. Stir in white chocolate chips.

5. Spread out dough in a 9-inch pan. Bake for 20 to 25 minutes. It is cooked when a toothpick comes out clean when inserted. Serve warm with ice cream and Maple Butter Sauce.

6. *Maple Butter Sauce:* In a pan, add real maple syrup and butter, cook over low heat until butter is melted. Stir in brown sugar until completely dissolved. If you desire, add walnuts.

Serves 4

*Arby's Apple Turnovers

Ingredients

1 package puff pastry sheets
4 large apples
1/2 cup sugar
1/4 teaspoon ground cinnamon
1 tablespoon cornstarch
1 teaspoon lemon juice

1. Peel, core then slice the apples.

2. Over low heat, in a medium saucepan, cook the apples with sugar, cornstarch, cinnamon and lemon juice. Stir often, until apples are tender.

3. Once tender, refrigerate until cool.

4. Preheat oven to 400 degrees F.

5. Unfold pastry on floured surface. Roll each sheet into a 12-inch square then cut into four 6-inch squares.

6. Place 1/4 cup of the apple mixture in the center of each square.

7. Brush the edges with water, then fold to form triangles. Be sure to seal the edges firmly with a fork.

8. Place on baking sheets. Bake 25 minutes or until golden.

9. Cool on wire rack.

Serving Suggestion:

In a small bowl, mix together 1/2 cup confectioners sugar and 1 tablespoon water. With a spoon, drizzle over the turnover, allow it to set before serving.

Serves 8

*Arby's Barbecue Sauce

The secret to Arby's signature sauce has finally been revealed!

Ingredients

1 cup ketchup
2 teaspoons water
2 teaspoons brown sugar
1/4 teaspoon Tabasco sauce
1/4 teaspoon garlic powder
1/4 teaspoon onion powder
1/4 teaspoon pepper

1/4 teaspoon salt
1/2 teaspoon worcestershire sauce

1. In a small saucepan, add all the ingredients and cook over medium heat. Stir until the sauce begins to boil, about 7 minutes.
2. Remove the pan from the heat. Allow to cool, covered.
3. Keep refrigerated, covered. Keeps for at least a month.

Serves 8

RecipeSecrets.net tip:
For an even greater kick, add more Tabasco sauce and Jalapeno.

*Arthur Treacher's Fried Fish

Ingredients

3 pounds fish fillets
2 cups all-purpose flour
3 cups pancake mix
3 cups club soda
1 tablespoon onion powder
1 tablespoon seasoned salt
1 egg

RecipeSecrets.net tip:
Use a meat thermometer to test the oil temperature. Always use caution when dropping the fillets into the hot oil.

1. Dip moistened fish pieces evenly but lightly in the flour. Dust off any excess flour and allow pieces to air dry on waxed paper, about 5 minutes.

2. Whip the pancake mix with the club soda to the consistency of buttermilk. It should be pourable, but not too thin and not too thick.

3. Beat in the onion powder and seasoned salt.

4. Dip floured fillets into batter and drop into 425 degrees F oil in a heavy saucepan.

5. Brown about 4 minutes per side.

6. Arrange on cookie sheet in 325 degrees F oven until all pieces have been fried.

Serves 4

*Bahama Breeze Jamaican Jerk Grilled Chicken Wings
So spicy and so flavorful!

Ingredients

5 pounds Chicken Wings whole, thawed
3 tablespoons Garlic, chopped
1 tablespoon Thyme, fresh chopped
1 teaspoon Allspice, ground
1 cup Water
1/8 cup Scallions, sliced
Jerk Seasoning (Dry), as needed

Jamaican Marinade
1/4 cup olive oil
2 tablespoons Jamaican Jerk seasoning

1/4 cup orange juice
1/4 cup rice wine vinegar
1 tablespoon dark Jamaican rum
1/2 cup chopped red onion
1/2 teaspoon creole seasoning
2 green onions, chopped
1 lime, juiced
2 cloves garlic, minced
1 habanero pepper, seeded and minced

1. Add the jerk marinade, garlic, thyme, allspice, water, and scallions in a large bowl and mix to evenly combine the ingredients.
2. Add the chicken wings to the marinade, cover with plastic wrap and place in the refrigerator.
3. Marinate the chicken wings for 16 to 24 hours before cooking.
4. Remove the wings from the marinade and place in a clean bowl. Make sure the wings are drained well after being removed from the marinade or the seasoning will not fully adhere to the wings.
5. Season the wings with the dry jerk seasoning and lay on a sheet pan with the wing tips face down.

6. Bake the wings at 350 degrees F for 20 a 25 minutes or until fully cooked.

7. Remove from oven and place in the refrigerator to chill to 40 degrees F. Pre-cooking the wings prevents flare-ups on the grill.

8. Place the chilled wings on the grill and grill for 2 1/2 - 3 minutes on each side on medium heat.

9. The skin of the wings should develop a crisp texture and a dark color. Make sure the wings are fully heated to 165 degrees F. Serve hot.

Serves 6-8

*Baskin Robbins Cheesecake Ice Cream

Ingredients

2 1/2 cups heavy whipping cream
1 1/4 cups sugar
2 beaten eggs
1 1/2 8-ounce packages cream cheese, softened
1/2 teaspoon finely shredded lemon peel
1 tablespoon lemon juice
1 teaspoon vanilla
Graham Crackers broken into bits

1. In a large saucepan combine 1 1/2 cups of the whipping cream, sugar, and eggs. Cook and stir over medium heat just until boiling.
2. In a large mixing bowl beat cream cheese with an electric mixer until smooth; slowly beat in hot mixture.
3. Cover and chill thoroughly.
4. Stir in remaining whipped cream, lemon peel, lemon juice, and vanilla.
6. Freeze in a 4-5 quart ice cream freezer according to the directions.
7. Fold in Graham Cracker bits.
8. Put into freezer container with a lid and let sit 4 hours in the freezer before serving.

Serves 8-10

*Bennigan's Broccoli Bites

Ingredients

3 eggs
6 ounces shredded Monterey Jack cheese
6 ounces shredded Colby cheese
1 (16 ounce) box frozen chopped broccoli, thawed, drained well
2 1/2 ounces bacon bits

1/2 ounce diced yellow onion
1 ounce all-purpose flour

Italian bread crumbs, as needed
Oil, for frying

1. Drain thawed broccoli.

2. Beat eggs in a mixing bowl.

3. Place all the ingredients into a bowl, except for the bread crumbs and stir together until thoroughly combined.

4. Refrigerate mixture for about 1 hour.

5. Heat about 4 cups oil in a fryer or pan to 350 degrees F.

6. Set up a shallow dish with bread crumbs.

7. Scoop about 1/2 ounce portion of the broccoli mixture into the bread crumbs. Form each portion into a ball and coat it evenly with the crumbs.

8. Place broccoli bites into the oil. Make sure they do not stick together. Fry for about one minute, then remove and place onto a dish lined with paper towels to drain.

Serve with Honey Mustard Dressing

Serves 4

*Bennigan's Honey Mustard Dressing

This goes great with Bennigan's Broccoli Bites

Ingredients

3/4 cup sour cream
1/3 cup mayonnaise
1/3 cup Dijon mustard
1/3 cup honey
1 tablespoon lemon juice

1. In a mixing bowl, combine sour cream, mayonnaise and mustard.
2. Mix well using a whisk.
3. Slowly pour in the honey and lemon juice, continue mixing until smooth.

RecipeSecrets.net tip:

Use this recipe as a dipping sauce or as a salad dressing !

Serves 4

*Bennigan's Hot Bacon Dressing

This warm dressing immerses crunchy bacon bits in a sweet, thickened vinaigrette.

Ingredients

2 ounce bacon drippings
1/4 pound red onion, diced fine
2 cups water
1/2 cup honey
1/2 cup red wine vinegar
2 tablespoon Dijon mustard
1 1/2 tablespoon cornstarch
1 tablespoon Tabasco sauce (optional)

1. Place the bacon grease in a saucepan over medium-high heat. Add the onions and sauté until the onions begin to blacken.

2. At the same time, in a mixing bowl combine the water, honey and red wine vinegar.

3. Using a whisk, mix the ingredients. Add the cornstarch and whisk well.

RecipeSecrets.net tip:

To reheat, use a double boiler.

4. After the onions have caramelized, add the Dijon mustard to the onions and mix together.

5. Add the water, vinegar, pepper, honey and cornstarch to the mustard and onions and mix. Continue stirring until mix thickens and comes to a boil. Remove from heat and store in refrigerator until needed.

Serves 8

*Bennigan's Linguini Diablo

Ingredients

Garlic Lemon Butter
1/2 cup butter, melted
2 teaspoons chopped garlic
1 1/2 teaspoon lemon juice
Marinara Sauce
3 tablespoons vegetable oil
8 ounces diced yellow onions
1 tablespoon chopped garlic
1 (28 oz.) can crushed tomatoes
3 1/2 tablespoons minced parsley
2 1/8 teaspoons dried oregano leaves
1 1/4 teaspoon dried basil leaves
1 whole bay leaf
1 1/2 teaspoon salt

1 lb linguini
1 tablespoon vegetable oil
12 scallops
12 large shrimp, peeled and deveined
10 clams
1 tablespoon parsley
1/3 cup Garlic Lemon Butter (recipe follows)
4 cups Marinara sauce (recipe follows)
Crushed Red pepper, to taste (optional)
1/4 cup grated Parmesan cheese
1 teaspoon parsley (for garnish)

RecipeSecrets.net tip:

When the pasta is cooked al dente, there should be a slight resistance in the center when the pasta is chewed.

1. In a large saucepan, heat oil over medium heat. Add onions. Saute until onions start to become soft and transparent, about 5 minutes.

2. Add garlic; cook 2 minutes, while stirring.

3. Add remaining ingredients to saucepan; stir. Bring sauce to boil.

4. Reduce heat to low, simmer uncovered for 30 minutes. Once cooked, remove bay leaf.

5. Cook linguini until al dente (approx. 8-10 minutes) drain well. Rinse and mix in vegetable oil to prevent sticking.

6. Mix the butter, garlic and lemon juice. Place garlic lemon butter in a large saute pan over medium-high heat. Be sure not to burn the garlic.

7. When butter starts sizzling, add the scallops, shrimp, and clams; saute for 5 minutes.

8. Add marinara sauce and stir the mixture to ensure even heating of all the ingredients.

9 Add linguini and toss until noodles are well covered with sauce. Continue to cook for another 2 minutes. Pour pasta into a large bowl and sprinkle with Parmesan cheese and parsley to garnish.

Serves 4

*Boston Market Cucumber Salad

Ingredients

2 medium cucumbers w/skin; 1/2" slices
1/4 red Spanish onion, 1/2" dice
1 large ripe tomato, dice
8 ounces oil & vinegar dressing
1 teaspoon dry dill weed
1/2 teaspoon dry parsley, mince
1/4 cup olive oil

1. Combine cucumbers with the rest of the ingredients in a plastic refrigerator container, cover tightly.
2. Allow salad to marinate for 24 hours in fridge before serving. Do not freeze.
3. Add salt and pepper to taste.

Serves 4-6

*Boston Market Meatloaf

Ingredients

1 egg
2 tablespoon sour cream
2 tablespoon ketchup
2 tablespoon flour
1 package of onion soup mix, dry
1 pound ground sirloin
2 tablespoon ketchup for coating
the meatloaf

1/3 cup spicy V-8 Juice

RecipeSecrets.net tip:
Freshly grated Parmesan cheese is an easy meatloaf flavor booster. Try adding 1/4 - 1/3 cup to your recipe.

1. Place the first 5 ingredients exactly as given into a blender. Blend briefly until smooth.

2. In medium bowl combine with beef. Mix well. Wet hands to shape into oval loaf.

3. Bake in greased 2 pound, foil, loaf tin at 400 degrees F for 45 minutes.

4. After first 15 minutes, coat top in ketchup and add the V-8 Juice around the loaf; return to bake the remaining 30 minutes.

Serves 2

*Boston Market Squash Casserole

Ingredients

4 1/2 cups zucchini, diced
4 1/2 cups yellow squash, diced
1 1/2 cup yellow onion, chopped
1 box Jiffy corn muffin mix
1 1/2 sticks of butter
8 ounces cheddar cheese

3 cubes chicken bouillon
1/2 teaspoon thyme
1 tablespoon parsley, chopped
1 teaspoon garlic, minced
1/2 teaspoon ground pepper
1 teaspoon salt

1. Prepare Jiffy mix as directed on the box, set aside to cool.
2. Preheat oven to 350 degrees F.
3. Place zucchini and yellow squash in a large saucepan and add water to cover.
4. Cook on medium low heat until tender, remove from heat.
5. Drain squash, reserve one cup of water for casserole.
6. In large sauce pan on medium low place the butter and saute the onions until the onions turn clear.
7. Add salt, pepper, thyme, and parsley.
8. Add chicken bouillon cubes and garlic to onions, stir and saute another minute.
9. Add drained squash and diced cheese, stir.
10. Crumble prepared corn bread in squash and pour the reserved cup of water and mix well.
11. Place squash mixture in a 13"x11" baking pan that has been sprayed with a non-stick spray.
12. Cover casserole. Bake for 50 to 60 minutes. Remove cover the last 20 minutes of baking time.

Serves 8

*Brooklyn Cafe Sun Dried Tomato Seared Scallops

Ingredients

10 sea scallops
salt and pepper, to taste
1 tablespoon garlic, minced
2/3 cup orange juice
1/4 cup & 2 tablespoon olive oil
1 tomato, diced
1 bunch fresh basil
1 tablespoon Lemon juice

3 zucchini, julienne
1/4 cup sun dried tomatoes

1. If sun dried tomatoes are moist, dry in 200 degrees F oven for about 15 minutes or until dry.

2. Chop sun-dried tomatoes in blender until it becomes a smooth powder, set aside.

3. Add basil, orange juice, and lemon juice to blender. Blend on moderate speed while drizzling 1/4 cup of olive oil in mixture.

4. Heat non-stick pan over medium heat, add 1 tbsp. Olive oil and garlic. Saute garlic for 15 seconds, do not burn, then add zucchini. Saute together, stirring frequently for 2 minutes until zucchini softens. Season with salt and pepper. Add tomatoes then turn off heat.

5. Heat another non-stick pan over medium-high heat. Season scallops with salt and pepper and with sun-dried tomato powder. Add 1 tbsp. Olive oil to pan and add scallops slowly.

6. Let cook for about 3 minutes, then flip. Let cook for another 2 minutes; transfer to a paper towel.

7. To serve, mound zucchini in the middle of two dinner plates. Place 5 scallops around each mound. Drizzle vinaigrette around the dish. Garnish with basil sprig and a sprinkling of tomato powder.

Serves 2

*Bullfish Shrimp & Cheese Grits

Ingredients

6 cups water
1/2 teaspoon salt
2 cups quick-cooking grits
1 cup grated sharp cheddar cheese
Pinch of ground nutmeg
Tabasco sauce, to taste
12 bacon slices, coarsely chopped
2 pounds large uncooked shrimp, peeled, deveined

1. Bring 6 cups water and salt to boil in a heavy large saucepan.
2. Whisk in grits. Reduce heat, cover and simmer until mixture is thick and grits are tender, stirring occasionally, about 10 minutes.
3. Whisk in 1 cup of cheese and nutmeg. Season to taste with hot pepper sauce. Cover and set aside.
4. Cook bacon in large skillet over medium heat until brown but not crisp. Transfer bacon to small bowl, using slotted spoon. Pour off half of drippings from skillet.
5. Add shrimp to same skillet and cook until just pink, about 2 minutes per side.
6. Transfer shrimp to plate, using slotted spoon.
7. Add mushrooms to same skillet and saute until tender, about 4 minutes.
8. Add green onions and garlic and saute 3 minutes.

9. Return shrimp and bacon to skillet. Mix in lemon juice. Season with salt, pepper and hot pepper sauce.

10. Bring grits to a simmer. Add water by tablespoons if grits are too thick.

11. Spoon grits onto plates. Spoon shrimp mixture over. Sprinkle with parsley and serve.

Serves 4

*California Pizza Kitchen Chicken Tequila Fettuccine

Ingredients

1 pound dry spinach fettuccine
1 1/4 pounds chicken breast, diced
1/2 cup chopped fresh cilantro
2 tablespoon chopped cilantro, garnish
2 tablespoons minced fresh garlic
2 tablespoons minced jalapeno pepper
  (seeds and veins removed)
3 tablespoons unsalted butter
  (reserve 1 tablespoon for saute)

1/2 cup chicken stock
1 1/2 cup heavy cream
2 tablespoons gold tequila
2 tablespoons lime juice
3 tablespoons soy sauce
1/4 medium red onion, thinly sliced
1/2 each medium red, yellow and
green bell pepper, sliced thin

1. Boil salted water to cook pasta; cook until al dente, 8 to 10 minutes for dry pasta, approximately 3 minutes for fresh. Pasta may be cooked ahead of time, rinsed and oiled and then reheated in boiling water.

2. Cook 1/3 cup cilantro, garlic and jalapeno in 2 tablespoons butter over medium heat for 4 to 5 minutes.

3. Add stock, tequila and lime juice. Bring to a boil, cook until reduced to a paste like consistency; set aside.

4. Pour soy sauce over diced chicken; set aside 5 minutes.

5. Meanwhile cook onion and peppers, stirring occasionally, with remaining butter over medium heat. When the vegetables become limp, add chicken and soy sauce; toss and add reserved tequila/lime paste and cream.

6. Bring the sauce to a boil; boil until chicken is cooked through and sauce is thick (about 3 minutes).

7. Toss with drained fettuccine and reserved cilantro.

Serves 4

*Carl Jr's Chicken Club

Ingredients

2 whole chicken breasts, boned and halved
1 cup teriyaki marinade
4 whole-wheat hamburger buns
8 slices bacon
1/4 cup mayonnaise
3/4 cup alfalfa sprouts

4 lettuce leaves
4 large tomato slices
4 slices Swiss cheese
Salt & Pepper, to taste

1. Marinate the chicken for at least 30 minutes in the teriyaki marinade.
2. Preheat your grill to medium heat.
3. Brown one side of each bun on the grill.
4. Cook the bacon in a pan until crunchy, then set aside.
5. Grill the chicken breasts about 5 minutes on each side, until cooked through.
6. Apply about 1/2 tablespoon of mayonnaise on the bun.
7. Divide the sprouts into 4 portions and place on each bottom bun.
8. Then, put a lettuce leaf, and a slice of tomato on top.
9. Put one chicken breast on top of the tomato.
10. Add a slice of Swiss cheese on the chicken, and 2 pieces of bacon.
11. Top with the other side of the bun.
12. Microwave for roughly 10 seconds to warm.

Serves 4

*Carrabba's Italian Grill Italian Butter

Ingredients

1/8 teaspoon oregano
1/8 teaspoon basil
1/8 teaspoon rosemary
1/8 teaspoon fresh ground pepper
dash of red pepper flakes
1 large clove of garlic (crushed)
2 to 3 Tablespoons extra virgin olive oil

1. Mix together dry spices.

2. Add crushed garlic to the spice mixture.

3. Put the spice mixture on a plate and pour olive oil over the spices.

4. Dip with your favorite hot bread.

Serves 1-2

*Carrabba's Italian Grill Meatballs

Ingredients

1/2 pound ground pork
1/2 pound ground veal
1/2 pound ground beef
2 large eggs, lightly beaten
1/4 cup grated Parmesan cheese
4 cloves garlic,
    finely chopped and sautéed
1/3 cup dry bread crumbs

1/4 cup finely chopped parsley
Salt and freshly ground pepper
1 cup pure olive oil

1. Combine all the ingredients in a medium bowl, except olive oil and season with salt and pepper to taste.
2. Heat the oil in large sauté pan over medium-high heat.
3. Roll the mixture into 1 1/2 inch balls and fry until brown on all sides, but not cooked through completely.
4. Remove with a slotted spoon to a plate lined with paper towels.
5. Put meatballs in an oven safe pan and bake at 375 degrees F for 20-25 minutes. You can also continue to cook these in a tomato sauce if desired.

Serves 4

*Cheesecake Factory Avocado Eggrolls

These are incredibly delicious!! For a low fat version, drizzle them with a little bit of olive oil and bake them in a 400 degrees F oven.

Ingredients

Dipping Sauce
1/4 cup olive oil
4 teaspoons white vinegar
1 teaspoon balsamic vinegar
1/2 teaspoon tamarind pulp
   or concentrate
1/2 cup honey (I use slightly less)
1 pinch turmeric
1/2 cup chopped cashews
2/3 cup fresh cilantro
2 garlic cloves
2 green onions
1 tablespoon sugar
1 teaspoon ground black pepper
1 teaspoon ground cumin

Eggrolls
1 large avocado, peeled, pitted, & diced
2 tablespoons sun-dried tomatoes, chopped
1 tablespoon finely chopped red onion
1/2 teaspoon fresh cilantro, chopped
1 dash salt
4 egg roll wraps
1 egg, beaten
Oil for deep-frying

Dipping Sauce

1. Combine vinegars, honey, tamarind, and saffron in a microwave safe bowl. Stir until tamarind is dissolved.

2. Microwave for 1 minute.

3. Using a food processor, puree tamarind mixture, cashews, cilantro, garlic, onions, sugar, pepper, and cumin.

4. Pour mixture into a bowl and stir in oil.

5. Cover and refrigerate until needed.

Egg Rolls

1. Stir together avocado, tomatoes, onion, cilantro, and salt.
2. Place some filling on the center of each egg roll wrapper.
3. Fold one corner up, 1/4 of the way over the filling. Brush the remaining corners and edges with beaten egg, roll up the left and right side, then fold top corner over all and press to seal.
4. Repeat with the remaining wrappers.
5. Deep-fry the egg rolls in 375 degrees F oil for 3-4 minutes, or until browned. Drain on paper towels.

Tip: If you wish, you can bake these instead of frying.

Serves 2-4

*Cheesecake Factory Banana Cream Cheesecake

Ingredients

20 vanilla sandwich cookies
1/4 cup margarine, melted
3 packages (8 ounces each) cream cheese, softened
2/3 cup sugar

2 tablespoons cornstarch
3 eggs
3/4 cup mashed bananas (about 2)
1/2 cup whipping cream
2 teaspoons vanilla

---

1. Preheat oven to 350 degrees F.

2. Place cookies in a blender; pulse until finely crushed.

3. Add margarine; process with pulses until combined.

4. Press mixture onto bottom of 10-inch springform pan; refrigerate.

RecipeSecrets.net tip:

Over-ripe bananas work great in this recipe!

5. Beat cream cheese in large bowl with electric mixer at medium speed until creamy. Add sugar and cornstarch; beat until blended. Add eggs, one at a time, continue beating. Mix in bananas, whipping cream, and vanilla.

6. Pour cream cheese mixture into crust.

7. Place pan on cookie sheet and bake 15 minutes. Reduce oven temperature to 200 degrees F and continue baking for 75 minutes or until center is almost set.

8. Loosen edge of cheesecake; cool completely on wire rack before removing rim of pan. Refrigerate, uncovered, 6 hours. Allow cheesecake to stand at room temperature 15 minutes before serving.

Serves 6-8

*Cheesecake Factory Crab Cakes

Ingredients

1/2 lb lump crabmeat
3 tablespoons plain breadcrumbs
(such as Progresso)
2 tablespoons mayonnaise
2 tablespoons minced green onions
(green part only)
2 tablespoons minced red bell peppers
pers
1/2 beaten egg
1 teaspoon minced fresh parsley
1 teaspoon Old Bay Seasoning

1/2 teaspoon prepared yellow mustard
tard
1/4 cup panko (Japanese breadcrumbs, available at Asian markets)
vegetable oil

1. Measure all the ingredients for the crab cakes, except the panko and vegetable oil, into a large bowl. Use a spatula to carefully fold the ingredients together. Avoid over-stirring.

2. Use your hands or a spoon to fill six cups of a clean muffin tin with equal amounts of the crab mixture. Press down a bit on each crab cake so that the top is flat but don't press too hard.

3. Cover the muffin tin with plastic wrap and pop it in the fridge for a couple hours to help the cakes stay together when they're browned in the oil.

4. After the crab cakes have chilled completely, heat about 1/4-inch of vegetable oil in large skillet over medium-low heat.

5. Fill a shallow bowl with the panko breadcrumbs.

6. Carefully turn the crab cakes out onto a plate.

7. Gently roll each crab cake around in the panko bread-crumbs. Each crab cake should be wearing a light coating of panko.

8. Test the oil by dropping a pinch of the panko crumbs into the oil. If it sizzles, the oil is ready. You can also use a thermometer to monitor the temperature.

9. Sauté the crab cakes in the hot oil for 1 1/2 to 3 minutes on each side or until the cakes are golden brown.

10. Drain crab cakes on paper towels or a rack, then serve them hot with a remoulade sauce.

Makes 6 Crab Cakes

*Cheesecake Factory Oreo Cheesecake

Ingredients

Filling
1 1/2 pound cream cheese
1 cup sugar
5 large eggs
1/4 teaspoon salt
2 teaspoon vanilla
1/4 cup flour
8 ounces sour cream
5 Oreo cookies (coarsely chopped for batter)
10 coarsely chopped Oreo cookies for topping

Crust
1 1/2 cup Oreo cookie crumbs
   (about 25 Oreo cookies finely chopped)
2 tablespoon melted butter
9" spring form pan
   (buttered on bottom and sides)

1. Mix melted butter with Oreo crumbs and press in the bottom of the spring pan and 1 1/2" up the sides, set aside.

2. All Ingredients must be at room temperature before beginning. Beat cream cheese with a mixer on low until fluffy.

3. Slowly add sugar and continue beating cream cheese until mixed well.

4. Add eggs one at a time and continue to beat until blended.

5. Measure the vanilla, salt and flour, pour into cream cheese and egg mixture and beat until smooth. Add the sour cream and beat.

6. Stir in the coarsely chopped oreo cookies with a spoon.

7. Pour cream cheese into the spring pan and place the nine coarsely chopped Oreo Cookies on to of the cream mixture.

8. Place pan on the top rack and in the middle of a pre-heated oven at 325 degrees F and bake for one hour and 15 minutes.

9. After that time, keep oven door open and let the cheese cake stay in the oven for one hour. Remove from oven and let cool enough to place in the refrigerator for 24 hours.

Serves 4-6

*Cheesecake Factory Pumpkin Ginger Cheesecake

Ingredients

Filling
1 cup heavy cream, chilled
24 ounces cream cheese, softened
1 1/2 cups granulated sugar
3 large eggs
1 1/2 cups mashed pumpkin
3/4 teaspoon ground cinnamon
3/4 teaspoon powdered ginger
3/8 teaspoon ground cloves

1/4 cup pecan halves

Crust
4 tablespoons butter
3/4 cup Graham Cracker crumbs
1/2 cup crushed gingersnaps
1 tablespoon brown sugar
1 teaspoon cinnamon

1. Preheat the oven to 325 degrees F.
2. Place the butter in a small saucepan and melt without burning.
3. Mix the graham cracker crumbs, gingersnaps, brown sugar and cinnamon in a bowl. Add the melted butter and mix together.
4. Line bottom and side of 10-inch springform pan with wax paper. Spray with nonstick spray. Press the crumb mixture into the bottom of the pan.
5. For the filling, pour the heavy cream into a medium bowl and beat just until soft peaks form. Refrigerate.
6. Beat the cream cheese with an electric mixer until fluffy. Slowly add the sugar, beating well. Add the eggs one at a time, and beat the mixture until it becomes fluffy.
7. Stir in the pumpkin, cinnamon, ginger and cloves.

8. Remove the whipped cream from the refrigerator and whisk to re-blend. Using a spatula, fold the whipped cream into the cream cheese-pumpkin mixture.

9. Pour the mixture into the prepared crust. Wrap one sheet of aluminum foil around the springform pan and press firmly.

10. Put wrapped pan in a baking pan and fill with hot water halfway up the spring from pan. Bake for about 65 minutes.

11. Cool to room temperature, then refrigerate for at least 3 hours. Place the pecan halves on top of the cheesecake before serving.

Serves 4

*Chili's Beef Fajitas

Juicy, marinated steak grilled to perfection! Served sizzling with onions and bell peppers.

Ingredients

1 1/2 pounds of sirloin steak
1 envelope dry onion soup mix
2 cups water
sauteed onion & green pepper
1 small can diced green chilies
flour tortillas
shredded cheddar cheese
salsa

RecipeSecrets.net tip:
Goes great with Mexican rice and refried beans.

1. Cut sirloin steak into bite size pieces.

2. Place in crockpot, with chili's, soup mix & water. Cook on low, 6-8 hours.

3. Chop onion & bell pepper in small stripes, saute in olive oil.

4. Warm tortillas in microwave.

5. Drain beef mixture. Place in center of tortillas, top with cheese, salsa & onion & pepper mix.

Serves 4

*Chili's Chocolate Chip Paradise Pie

Ingredients

Filling:
1/2 cup flour
1/4 cup granulated sugar
3/4 teaspoon baking powder
1/3 cup milk
1 tablespoon oil
1 teaspoon vanilla extract
1/3 cup semi-sweet or milk chocolate chips

1/4 cup shredded coconut
1/4 cup crushed walnuts or almonds

Crust:
1/3 cup Graham Cracker crumbs
3 tablespoon granulated sugar
3 tablespoon butter
1/3 cup chocolate chips

Crust

1. Preheat oven to 350 degrees F.
2. Melt butter and combine with the Graham Cracker crumbs and sugar.
3. Press into bottom of a 1 quart casserole dish. Top evenly with chocolate chips.
4. Bake for 5 minutes until chocolate is melted. Spread melted chips out evenly over crust.

Filling

1. Combine dry ingredients in large mixing bowl.
2. Add milk, oil and vanilla and stir until smooth. Stir in chocolate chips, coconut, and nuts. Pour into crust.
3. Bake, uncovered, for 35 to 40 minutes, until a wooden pick comes out clean.
4. Serve warm with ice cream, hot fudge and caramel.

Serves 4

*Chili's Margarita Grilled Chicken

Ingredients

4 boneless, skinless chicken breasts
1 cup Margarita Mix liquid
1/4 cup tequila
1 tablespoon minced garlic
freshly ground black pepper, to taste
Salt, to taste

1. Combine margarita mix, tequila and garlic in a dish with the chicken breasts and let marinate for 2 hours in refrigerator. When ready to prepare drain and season with black pepper to taste.
2. Preheat your grill to medium high temperature.
3. Spray grill with olive oil and braise chicken breast until done on each side.
4. Serve chicken breast with black beans, Mexican rice and some fresh salsa.

Serves 4

*Chili's Nacho Burger

Ingredients

Pico de Gallo:
2 tomatoes, diced
1/2 cup diced Spanish onion
2 tablespoon chopped jalapeno
2 tablespoon fresh cilantro, finely minced
1 tablespoon lime juice
pinch of salt
Guacamole:
1 large avocado
2 tablespoon sour cream
1/2 cup diced tomato
1/4 tablespoon diced jalapeno
1/4 tablespoon chopped fresh cilantro
1/4 tablespoon lemon juice
1/8 tablespoon salt

Chili Queso:
3 ounces ground beef
1 tablespoon all-purpose flour
pinch of salt
pinch of ground black pepper
16 ounce bottle Cheez Whiz
2 tablespoon milk
1/8 tablespoon chili powder
1/8 tablespoon cumin
1/8 tablespoon paprika
Burger:
2 pound ground beef
4 large sesame seed buns
2 cups lettuce, shredded
2 tablespoon mayonnaise
1 green onion, chopped
About 20 tortilla chips
2-3 fresh jalapenos, sliced

1. Make the pico de gallo by mixing all of the ingredients in a small bowl. Cover and chill in the refrigerator until needed.

2. To make the guacamole, in a small bowl, mash up the avocado, but leave some un-mashed chunks. Add in the remaining ingredients for the guacamole. Refrigerate covered until needed.

3. For the queso, in a bowl, mix together ground beef, flour, and a pinch each of salt, black pepper, and chili

powder. Use your hands to mix the dry ingredients into the beef. Brown the beef in a pan over medium heat for 5 minutes, drain fat and set aside.

4. Melt the Cheez Whiz over low heat with 2 tablespoons of milk. Once combined, add the remaining ingredients. Heat until cheese is smooth, stir so it does not burn. Cover saucepan and set aside.

5. Preheat a large frying pan over medium heat. Butter each bun and brown buns face-down in the pan.

6. Make 4 burger patties and cook 7 minutes on each side or until desired doneness.

7. Assemble burger with lettuce, queso, crumbled tortilla chips, green onions, mayo, pico de gallo, guacamole and jalapeno slices as desired.

Serves 4

*Chili's Salsa

Ingredients

14 1/2 oz can tomatoes and green chills
14 1/2 oz can whole peeled tomatoes plus the juice
1 tablespoon jalapeños (canned, diced, not pickled)
1 teaspoon jalapeños (canned, diced, not pickled)
1/4 cup diced onion
3/4 teaspoon garlic salt, to taste
1/2 teaspoon cumin, or more to taste
1/4 teaspoon sugar, to taste

1. Place jalapeños and onions in a food processor; pulse for just a few seconds.
2. Add both cans of tomatoes, salt, sugar and cumin.
3. Process all ingredients until well blended, but do not puree. You want the salsa to be chunky.
4. Serve immediately or refrigerate.

Serves 4

*Church's Fried Chicken

Ingredients

1 tablespoon sugar	1 envelope Italian dressing mix
1 1/2 cups self-rising flour	1 envelope onion soup mix
1/2 cup cornstarch	1 chicken (Cut into Pieces)
3 teaspoon seasoned salt	2 eggs, mix with
2 teaspoon paprika	1/4 cup cold water
1/2 teaspoon baking soda	1 cup corn oil (for frying)
1/2 cup biscuit mix	

1. Combine first set of ingredients in a 4-cup bowl. Mix to blend ingredients thoroughly.

2. Dip the chicken pieces in egg mixture and then into dry coating mix and repeat so each piece is double coated.

RecipeSecrets.net tip:
Always use caution when cooking with hot oil.
Consider baking instead of frying for a healthier alternative.

3. Pre-heat the oil in a heavy skillet. Brown pieces skin-side down for 5 minutes. Use medium high heat.

4. Turn and brown underside of pieces a few minutes. Transfer to an oiled pan. Cover with foil, sealing it on only 3 sides of pan.

5. Bake at 350 degrees F for about 45 to 50 minutes. Remove foil, then bake another 5 minutes until the coating is crisp.

Serves 4-6

*Claim Jumper's Cheese Potatocakes

Ingredients

Potatocakes
4 medium red potatoes, with skin
1/4 cup shredded cheddar cheese
1/4 cup shredded monterey jack cheese
2 tablespoon shredded parmesan cheese
1 green onion, chopped
1/2 teaspoon minced fresh cilantro
1/2 teaspoon salt
1/4 teaspoon ground black pepper
1/4 teaspoon garlic powder
Breading
2/3 cup unseasoned breadcrumbs

1/3 cup all-purpose flour
1/2 teaspoon dried dill
1 egg, beaten
1 cup milk
Herbed Ranch Salsa
1/2 cup sour cream
1/4 cup seeded and diced tomato
2 tablespoons minced onion
1 tablespoon white vinegar
1 teaspoon fresh minced cilantro
1/2 teaspoon salt
1/4 teaspoon ground black pepper
pinch dried dill

1. Boil potatoes for 25 minutes, until soft but not mushy.
2. Make the herbed ranch salsa by mixing all of the ingredients in a bowl. Cover and refrigerate the sauce until needed.
3. Drain the potatoes and mash them with the skin on in a medium bowl until they become small chunks. Add the remaining ingredients to the potatoes and mix.
4. Mix the breadcrumbs with flour and dill in a large bowl.
5. Put the beaten egg and milk in another bowl.
6. Using your hands, measure about 1/3 cup of the potato mixture and shape it into a 3 inch patty. Coat the potato mixture with the breading mixture, then dip into the egg and milk, then back into the breading. Cover the entire surface of the potatocake with the breading. Set it on a plate and repeat. Cover and chill the breaded potatocakes for about an hour, to help

bind.

7. Heat up 3 cups of oil in a skillet over medium-low heat. Fry the potatocakes in the oil for 3 minutes or until brown. Drain on paper towels.

8. Serve potatocakes with the herbed ranch salsa.

Makes 6 potatocakes

*Coney Island Chili Dog Sauce

Ingredients

1 pound ground beef, lean
1 small onion, chopped
2 tablespoon prepared yellow mustard
2 tablespoon vinegar
2 tablespoon sugar
1 tablespoon water
1 teaspoon worcestershire sauce

1/4 teaspoon celery seed
1/4 teaspoon Tabasco sauce
1/4 cup catsup
(Use enough to keep mixture loose)

1. In salted skillet, over medium heat, brown ground beef with onion, breaking up meat with fork to crumble fine. Drain off fat.

2. Add mustard, vinegar, sugar, water, Worcestershire sauce, celery seed, and Tabasco sauce. Mix well. Add enough catsup to keep mixture loose.

3. Reduce heat to low, and simmer (uncovered), for 35 to 40 minutes. Makes enough sauce for six to eight medium hot dogs.

Serves 6-8

*Coney Island Spuds

Ingredients

3 large baking potatoes
3/4 pound ground beef
1 15-ounce can of sloppy joe sauce
1 8-ounce container sour cream dip with chives

1. Scrub potatoes with a brush and prick skin with a fork.
2. Bake in a 425 degrees F oven for 40 to 60 minutes or until tender.
3. Brown beef in a skillet and drain.
4. Stir in sloppy joe sauce. Bring to a boil and reduce heat. Cover and simmer 5 minutes.
5. Stir in half of the sour cream dip and 1/4 cup of water. Heat thoroughly. Do not boil.
6. Quarter potatoes lengthwise. Spoon meat mixture over potatoes. Top with remaining dip.

Serves 4

*Country Fair Funnel Cakes

Ingredients

2 eggs, lightly beaten
1 1/2 cups milk
1/4 cup packed brown sugar
2 cups flour
1 1/2 teaspoon baking powder
1/4 teaspoon salt
oil for deep-frying
confectioner's sugar - for dusting

1. In a bowl, combine the eggs, milk, and brown sugar. Combine flour, baking powder, and salt; beat into egg mixture until smooth.
2. In an electric skillet or deep-fat fryer, heat oil to 375 degrees F.
3. Cover the bottom of a funnel spout with your finger; ladle 1/2 cup batter into funnel. Holding the funnel several inches above the skillet, release finger and move the funnel in a spiral motion until all of the batter is released.
4. Fry for 2 minutes on each side or until golden brown. Drain on paper towels. Repeat with remaining batter.
5. Dust with confectioners' sugar; serve warm.

Serves 4-6

*Cracker Barrel Baby Limas

Ingredients

I chicken bouillon cube
I cup water
I strip bacon
2 pinches red pepper flakes
I clove garlic, peeled and lightly smashed
I 16 ounce bag frozen baby limas

1. Bring water and bouillon to boil.

2. Add all ingredients. Cover pan and turn heat to simmer. Cook at least 25 minutes.

3. Salt and pepper to taste. Serve.

RecipeSecrets.net tip:

If water is needed, only add boiling water.

Serves 4

*Cracker Barrel Banana Pudding

This recipe is classic just like grandma used to make. For a shorter version of this recipe you can buy 2 boxes of flavored banana pudding from your favorite supermarket and follow the directions on the box. Then start following the recipe directions from line 6.

Ingredients

1 1/2 cup sugar	2 teaspoons vanilla
1/2 cup flour -plus-	4 tablespoons butter
2 tablespoons flour	1 (12 ounce) box Vanilla Wafers
1/2 teaspoon salt	7 bananas (sliced about 1/3" thick)
4 cups whole milk	1 (9" x 13") greased cake pan
5 large egg yolks (beaten)	1 large container whipped topping

1. In a large sauce pan on medium low heat combine sugar, flour, salt, and milk. Stir until completely blended.

2. When mixture begins to boil, cook for 2 minutes, stirring constantly as it begins to thicken.

3. Remove from heat and add 1/2 cup of hot mixture to beaten eggs and stir until blended.

4. Place pudding mixture back on stove on medium heat and add egg mixture, continue cooking for 3 minutes.

5. After 3 minutes turn heat off, add butter and vanilla, beat until blended.

6. Remove from heat and let cool for about ten minutes.

7. Spray your pan with non stick spray and arrange vanilla wafers to cover the bottom and sides of baking pan.

8. Slice bananas and cover the wafers with bananas. Pour pudding in pan, covering bananas and wafers.

9. Cool banana pudding in refrigerator. When pudding has set, cover with whipped topping.

Serves 6

*Cracker Barrel Cherry Chocolate Cobbler

Ingredients

1 1/2 cup flour
1/2 cup sugar
2 teaspoons baking powder
1/2 teaspoon salt
1/4 cup butter
1 (6 oz.) pkg. semisweet chocolate morsels

1/4 cup milk
1 egg
1 (21 oz.) can cherry pie filling
1/2 cup nuts, finely chopped

1. Preheat oven to 350°F.
2. In large bowl, combine flour, sugar, baking powder, salt and butter; cut with pastry blender until crumbs are size of large peas.
3. Using a double boiler, melt the semisweet chocolate.
4. Remove from heat and cool slightly at room temperature (about 5 minutes).
5. Add milk and egg to melted chocolate and mix well.
6. Blend chocolate into flour mixture.
7. Spread cherry pie filling in bottom of 2-quart casserole. Drop chocolate batter randomly over cherries. Sprinkle with nuts
8. Bake at 350°F for 40 - 45 minutes. Serve hot.

Serves 6

*Cracker Barrel Fried Apples

Ingredients

6 tart apples, sliced
1 teaspoon lemon juice
1/4 cup bacon drippings
1/4 cup brown sugar
1/8 teaspoons salt
1 teaspoon cinnamon
1 dash nutmeg

1. In a large skillet, melt bacon drippings.
2. Pour apples over the bottom of the skillet.
3. Pour lemon juice over them, then brown sugar, then salt.
4. Cover and cook over low heat for 15 minutes until apples are tender and juicy.
5. Sprinkle with cinnamon and nutmeg.

Serves 6

*Dairy Queen Ice Cream

Ingredients

I envelope powdered unflavored gelatin
1/4 cup cold water
I cup whole milk
I cup sugar
I tsp. vanilla extract
1/4 tsp salt
I 1/2 cups heavy whipping cream

1. Sprinkle gelatin over water and let stand 5 minutes.
2. Meanwhile, heat milk to almost a simmer on stovetop.
3. Remove from heat.
4. Stir in sugar, vanilla and salt with a wire whisk until completely dissolved, at least 2 minutes.
5. Stir into gelatin mixture and let cool.
6. Stir in whipping cream. Cover and refrigerate 6 hours.
7. Transfer to ice cream machine and process for about 20 minutes until creamy.

Serves 2

RecipeSecrets.net tip:

You can get creative with this recipe by adding your favorite topping: gummy bears, m&m's, chocolate syrup or fresh strawberries.

*Dairy Queen Onion Rings

Ingredients

2 Vidalia onions
2 cups flour
2 cups fine cracker crumbs
2 cups white corn meal
2 cups buttermilk
1 cup water
4 cups oil (enough for your deep fryer)

1. Slice onions 1/2 inch thick and only use the larger rings.

2. In a large bowl combine buttermilk and water.

3. In another bowl combine the corn meal and cracker crumbs.

4. Put the flour in another bowl.

5. Take each ring and coat them with flour then with buttermilk, and then coat with corn meal mixture.

6. Carefully drop each ring into hot oil and fry until golden.

7. Drain on paper towels.

Serves 2

*Denny's Chicken Fried Steak

Ingredients

4 cubed steaks	1/3 cup cooking oil
corn oil	seasoning salt and pepper, to taste
seasoning salt	
2-3 tablespoons red wine or juice	
2 cups Bisquick	
1/4 pound melted butter	

1. The night before, put the steaks in a single layer on a dish. Brush them on both sides with an even coating of corn oil. Dust them on both sides with a generous amount of seasoning salt. Drizzle each steak with wine or juice. Seal the dish in foil or plastic wrap and refrigerate it for about 24 hours prior to preparing the final dish.

2. Remove the steaks from the fridge and coat both sides well in the Bisquick mix. Season with salt and pepper, to taste.

3. Preheat the oven to 375 degrees F.

4. Combine the butter with the oil in a large skillet until melted.

5. Place the steaks in the skillet. Brown both sides of each steak, until crispy.

6. Transfer to a baking dish and seal in foil. Bake at 375 degrees F for about 30 minutes.

RecipeSecrets.net tip:

Try making this recipe with a chicken cutlet instead of beef. Serve with mashed potatoes and fresh steamed vegetables.

Serves 4

*Dollywood Dipped Chocolate Chip Cookies

Ingredients

2 1/4 cups all-purpose flour
1 teaspoon baking soda
1 teaspoon salt
1 cup butter, softened
3/4 cup granulated sugar
3/4 cup brown sugar, firmly packed
1 teaspoon vanilla extract
2 eggs

12 ounces semi-sweet chocolate chips

Chocolate Dip
1 (6 ounce) bag semi-sweet chocolate morsels
1 (6 ounce) bag white chocolate morsels
vegetable oil

1. Preheat oven to 375 degrees F.
2. In a small bowl, combine flour, baking soda, and salt; set aside.
3. In a large bowl combine butter, sugar, and vanilla extract; mix until creamy.
4. Beat in eggs. Gradually add flour mixture. Stir in 12 ounces semi-sweet chips.
5. Drop by level teaspoonfuls onto ungreased baking sheet. Bake 9-11 minutes. Cookies should still be soft when removed from oven. Place on cooling racks.
6. In separate small saucepans, melt bags of semi-sweet and white chocolate morsels.
7. Add a small amount of vegetable oil to each saucepan.
8. Dip each cookie halfway in dark chocolate and return to rack to cool.
9. After cooled, dip the other half in the white chocolate. Allow to cool.

Serves 8-10

*El Pollo Loco Beans

El Pollo Loco, pronounced "L-Po-yo Lo-co" is Spanish for "The Crazy Chicken." This restaurant started out in 1975 as a roadside chicken stand in Mexico. It's success spread rapidly throughout Mexico and into the US. Billed as "a wholesome, delicious alternative to traditional fast food faire."

Ingredients

1/4 cup	corn oil
5	whole serrano chilis
2 tsp	ground serrano chilis
1	can pinto beans, (28 ounces) drain
3/4 cup	water

RecipeSecrets.net tip:
A perfect side for tacos, fajitas, quesadillas and your other favorite Spanish dishes.

1. Heat oil in large saucepan.

2. Add whole chilis. Cook until tender.

3. Add ground chilis, beans and water. Stir well.

4. Bring to boil, reduce heat. Simmer 17 minutes, stirring often.

Serves 4

*Entenmann's Apple Crumb Cake

Ingredients

1/3 cup butter	1 package active dry yeast
4 Granny Smith apples	3/4 cup water
3/4 cup sugar	1/3 cup butter
1 teaspoon lemon peel	1 egg
1/2 teaspoon cinnamon	1 teaspoon lemon peel
1/8 teaspoon mace	3/4 cup chopped pecans
1/3 cup currants	6 tablespoon flour
2 1/2 cups flour	1/4 cup confectioners sugar
3 tablespoon sugar	3 tablespoon butter
1/2 teaspoon salt	1/4 teaspoon cinnamon

RecipeSecrets.net tip: You can substitute fresh fruit topping such as raspberry, strawberry or blueberry

1. Melt butter in large skillet. Pare, core and slice apples to 1/2" pieces. Add apples to butter and cook, stirring, 8 minutes until tender. stir in sugar, peel, cinnamon, mace and currants. Cook 15 minutes, stirring until thickened. Cool.

2. In large bowl, combine 1 cup flour, sugar, salt and yeast. In small saucepan, combine water and butter. Heat on low flame until 120 degrees F. Gradually add to dry ingredients. Beat 2 minutes. Beat in egg, peel and 3/4 cup flour. With mixer, beat 2 minutes. Stir in remaining flour.

3. Cover, let rest 20 minutes. Grease 2 baking sheets. Put half the dough on well floured work surface, roll to 14"x12". Place on sheet. Spread 1/2 filling lengthwise

down center of the dough. Starting about 3/4" for fill-ing, cut 1" wide strips diagonally from filling to edges of dough.

4. Alternately fold opposite strips of dough at angles across filling. Fold ends over filling. Brush large piece of waxed paper with vegetable oil. Loosely cover sheet.

5. Top with plastic wrap. Refrigerate 2 hours. Uncover, let stand at room temperature 10 minutes. Preheat oven to 375 degrees F. Combine rest of ingredients for topping. Sprinkle over loaves.

6. Bake 25 minutes until lightly browned. Remove from sheet. Let cool.

Makes 2 Cakes

*Entenmann's Pound Cake

Ingredients

1/2 pound butter
2 cups powdered sugar
3 large eggs
1 2/3 cup all purpose flour
1 tablespoon vanilla extract or lemon

1. Preheat oven to 325 degrees F.
2. Grease an 8-1/2" Pyrex loaf dish.
3. Cream butter with sugar on high speed of mixer for 5 minutes.
4. Add 1 egg and then a little flour, continue beating for 2 minutes. Add 2nd egg and half of remaining flour and beat 2 minutes. Add 3rd egg, rest of flour and extract, beating 2 minutes.
5. Spread batter evenly in prepared loaf dish.
6. Bake 65 minutes or until tester inserted into center comes out clean.
7. Cool in baking dish on wire rack 30 minutes.

Makes 1 loaf

*Hard Rock Cafe Baked Potato Soup

Ingredients

3 pounds pork shoulder
1 quart hot water
1 quart apple-cider vinegar
1/2 cup Tabasco sauce
1/2 cup granulated sugar

1. Fry bacon until crisp. Chop bacon and save the drippings.
2. Cook onions in the bacon drippings over medium-high heat until soft, about 3 minutes.
3. Add flour, stirring to prevent lumps. Cook for 4 minutes.
4. Add chicken stock slowly, whisk to prevent lumps, until liquid thickens.
5. Reduce heat to simmer and add potatoes, cream, chopped bacon, parsley, garlic, basil, salt, pepper sauce and black pepper. Simmer 10 minutes; Do not boil.
6. Add grated cheese and green onions. Heat until cheese melts. Garnish as desired with chopped bacon, parsley, grated cheese.

Serves 6

*Hard Rock Cafe Pulled Pork

Ingredients

8 slices bacon
1 cup diced yellow onions
2/3 cup Flour
6 cups hot chicken stock
4 cups peeled and diced baked
Potatoes
2 cups heavy cream
1/4 cup chopped parsley
1 1/2 teaspoon granulated garlic
1 1/2 teaspoon dried basil

1 1/2 teaspoon salt
1 1/2 teaspoon red pepper sauce
1 1/2 teaspoon coarse black pepper
1 cup grated cheddar cheese
1/4 cup diced green onions(white
part)
additional chopped bacon
grated cheese
chopped parsley for garnish

1. In a large bowl, combine apple-cider vinegar, Tabasco sauce, sugar and hot water. Stir until sugar is dissolved. Pour marinade over pork, cover and refrigerate overnight.

2. Remove pork from marinade and place in a baking pan. Save the marinade. Cook in a preheated 450 degrees F oven until browned.

3. Pour some marinade over pork, lower temperature to 300 degrees F, cover and slow-roast for an additional two hours or until meat pulls away from the bone easily.

Serves 6

*Hardee's Cinnamon "Flake" Biscuits

Ingredients

Biscuit Dough

2 1/2 cups	Bisquick
2 tablespoon sugar	
1/2 cup	dark raisins
1/3 cup	buttermilk
1/2 cup	tonic water
1/2 tsp	vanilla

Mixture

1 small box   bran flakes

1 tablespoon cinnamon
2 tablespoon brown sugar, packed
2 tablespoon butter, melted

Icing

2 tablespoons butter, melted
1 teaspoon vanilla
2 tablespoons sour cream
1 pinch salt
1 1/2 cups powdered sugar

1. Empty the box of cereal into blender. Add in cinnamon and brown sugar and pulse on high speed, for about 3 seconds or until crumbled, but not powdered.

2. Empty into small bowl. Stir in melted butter with a fork. Set aside.

3. Using a 2-quart mixing bowl. Stir Bisquick together with sugar and raisins.

4. Put buttermilk, tonic water and vanilla into a measuring cup, and pour into Bisquick mixture. Use a fork to mix until all of the liquid is absorbed. Then knead in the bowl with hands, dipping into additional Bisquick, to make dough smooth and no longer stick.

5. Break dough up into 5 portions in the bowl - sprinkle the "flake" mixture over the dough and then work it in until most of it is evenly distributed throughout the dough.

6. Divide dough into 12 equal parts and shape each into 1/2" thick patty, arranging close together in 2 greased 8" round layer cake pans. Bake at 400 degrees F for 25 minutes or until golden. Remove pan to wire rack and coat tops with icing.

Icing:

1. In small bowl with electric mixer on high speed, beat 2 tablespoons melted butter, 1 teaspoon vanilla, 2 tablespoons sour cream, dash of salt and 1-1/2 cups powdered sugar until smooth.

Serves 4-6

*Hooters Buffalo Shrimp

Looking for an appetizer with some kick? Try this alternative to hot wings.

Ingredients

Buffalo Sauce
1/4 cup hot sauce
1/4 cup butter
1/8 teaspoon paprika
1 pinch black pepper
1 pinch garlic powder
1/8 teaspoon cayenne pepper

Shrimp
12 uncooked large shrimp,
  peeled and deveined
1 egg, beaten
1/2 cup milk
1 cup all-purpose flour

1. Over medium heat, add the ingredients for the buffalo sauce to a small saucepan, heat until butter is melted. Cover, and keep warm.
2. Beat the egg and milk in a small bowl.
3. Place flour in a bowl or a large zip bag.
4. Coat half of the shrimp with egg mixture, then toss them in the flour.
5. Repeat the process with the rest of the shrimp. Make sure they are all coated with flour.
6. Refrigerate about 5 minutes and pre-heat the deep fryer to 375 degrees F.
7. Deep fry for 8 to 10 minutes, until shrimp is cooked and golden. Remove, drain, and toss with Buffalo Sauce.

* *If you like, you can remove the tails before breading to make popcorn shrimp.*

RecipeSecrets.net tip:

Serve with blue cheese or for an added kick, spicy chipotle mayo

Serves 2 to 4

*IHOP Banana Nut Pancakes

Ingredients

Pancakes:
1/4 cup vegetable oil
1 1/4 cups all-purpose flour
1 1/2 cups buttermilk
1 egg
2 tablespoon sugar
1 1/2 teaspoons baking powder
1 teaspoon baking soda
1/2 teaspoon banana extract

1/4 teaspoon salt
1/2 cup chopped pecans
1 banana
Banana Syrup:
1/2 cup corn syrup
1/2 cup sugar
1/2 cup water
1/4 teaspoon banana extract
1/4 teaspoon vanilla extract

1. To repare the banana syrup, stir corn syrup, sugar and water together in a small saucepan over high heat. Remove from heat once it boils. Mix in banana and vanilla extract.

2. Use an electric mixer to mix all the ingredients for the pancakes except for the banana and pecans. The batter should be smooth.

3. Pre-heat griddle to medium heat, coat with nonstick spray.

4. Use a ladle to pour 1/4 cup of batter onto the griddle and allow the batter to spread out. Immediately sprinkle about 3/4 tablespoon of the pecans into the center of each pancake so that the pecans are set in place. Cook the pancakes for 1 to 2 minutes on each side. The edges will lift slightly and the surfaces should be lightly browned.

5. Slice the banana, and serve it on top of a stack of 3 pancakes. Serve with whipped cream and the remaining chopped pecans on top.

Serves 4

*IHOP Swedish Pancakes

Swedish Pancakes can be served for breakfast or dessert, but Swedes prepare them for supper.

Ingredients

3 eggs
1 cup milk
1 1/2 cup sifted flour
1 tablespoon sugar
1/2 teaspoon salt
1/2 cup cream (or milk)

2 tablespoon butter, melted
Confectioners sugar
2 cup lingonberry sauce

1. Beat eggs very well.
2. Sift together the flour, salt and sugar.
3. Add half the milk and fold in flour, sifted with sugar and salt.
4. Then add remaining milk, cream and butter. Add more milk if the consistency is too thick.
5. Using a hot griddle or crepe pan, ladle the batter onto the surface creating a 5 inch diameter. These pancakes should be thin and will only need a minute or two on each side to brown.
6. Place 2 tablespoons of lingonberry (Swedish cranberries) sauce on center of pancake and roll up like jelly roll.
7. Serve sprinkled with confectioners sugar.

Serves 4

*Ikea Swedish Meatballs

Ingredients

1 small onion, finely chopped
1 tablespoon vegetable oil
2/3 pound lean ground beef
1/3 pound ground lean pork
1/2 cup breadcrumbs
1 cup milk
1 egg, lightly beaten

1 teaspoon salt
1 teaspoon black pepper
1/4 teaspoon ground allspice
1 tablespoon vegetable oil (for frying)
1 (10 ounce) can beef gravy
1/2 cup cream

1. Saute onions in one tablespoon of oil until soft and clear. Set aside.
2. Combine breadcrumbs with milk, let soak for 10 minutes.
3. In a large bowl, combine onions, breadcrumbs, milk egg, meat and seasonings. Mix well. Form tablespoons of the meat mixture into small meatballs.
4. Over medium heat, fry meatballs in one tablespoon of oil until brown on all sides.
5. In a small saucepan, combine gravy and cream; heat through but do not boil.
6. Serve meatballs with gravy and boiled potatoes. Also good with pasta of your choice.

Serves 4-6

*Jack In The Box Taco

Ingredients

1 pound ground beef
1 tablespoon potato flakes
1/3 cup refried beans
1/4 teaspoon salt
2 tablespoon chili powder
pinch cayenne pepper
1/4 cup mild taco sauce
12 soft corn tortillas

3 cups cooking oil, Crisco brand
6 slices American cheese
1 head lettuce, shredded

1. Brown the beef over low heat, then drain the fat. Add the refried beans and use a spoon to mash the whole beans to create a smooth texture. Add in the potato flakes and stir until combined.

2. Add the salt, chili powder, cayenne and 2 tablespoons of taco sauce to the mixture. Remove from the heat.

3. In another skillet heat 1/4 inch of oil.

4. Heat the tortillas slightly in the microwave. Spread some of the beef on the center of each tortilla. Fold the tortillas over and press together so that the filling holds the sides together. Carefully drop each taco into the hot oil and fry on both sides until crisp. Remove the tacos from the oil and place them on some paper towels to drain the oil.

5. Carefully open the taco and add 1/2 slice American cheese and some lettuce. Top with 1/2 teaspoon of the taco sauce or salsa.

Serves 6

*Johnny Carino's 5 Cheese Chicken Fettuccine

Asiago cheese is an italian cheese, whose flavor is reminiscent of sharp Cheddar and Parmesan.

Ingredients

8 ounces Alfredo sauce
1/2 teaspoon black pepper
1/2 teaspoon each salt, pepper, & garlic salt
3 ounces chicken, cooked & sliced
1/8 cup Parmesan cheese
1/8 cup Romano cheese
1/8 cup Mozzarella cheese
1/8 cup Provolone cheese
1/8 cup Asiago cheese
10 ounces cooked fettuccine

1. Into a warm saute pan, combine alfredo sauce, black pepper, spice mixture, and chicken. Saute until the sauce begins to boil and the chicken is heated.

2. As sauce continues to boil, begin to mix in cheese until a dense smooth sauce is formed.

3. Remove from heat, add pasta, toss, and serve.

Serves 2

*KFC Buttermilk Biscuits

Ingredients

2 cups all-purpose flour
1/4 teaspoon baking soda
1 tablespoon baking powder
3/4 cup buttermilk
1 teaspoon salt
6 tablespoon shortening

1. Sift the dry ingredients in a large bowl.
2. Cut in the shortening with a pastry cutter until a coarse texture is obtained.
3. Add buttermilk and knead.
4. The dough should be soft but not sticky: if it is, add a little more flour. Knead for 1 minute, wrap in wax paper and refrigerate for at least 20 minutes.
5. Preheat the oven to 450 degrees F.
6. Roll out the dough 1/2 inch thick on a lightly floured surface and cut with a biscuit cutter or the top of a cup.
7. Transfer biscuits to a dark baking sheet and bake until brown,
10-12 minutes.

Serves 6

*Little Debbie Bars

Ingredients

I box devil's food cake mix with pudding
Filling:
5 tablespoons flour
I cup milk
1/2 teaspoon salt
I cup sugar
1/2 cup shortening

1/2 cup butter
I teaspoon vanilla

Frosting:
1/2 cup sugar
6 tablespoons milk
6 tablespoons butter/margarine

1. Open I box devil's food cake mix with pudding in mix. Mix as directed.
2. Grease two jellyroll pans. Divide batter, half in each pan. Bake 12 minutes.
3. For filling, blend flour, salt and milk.
4. Heat until thickened, then cool.
5. Cream sugar, shortening and butter at high speed, gradually adding cooled mixture. Beat at high speed 7-8 minutes.
6. Spread on one pan of cooled cake. Invert other jellyroll pan with cake on top.
7. For the frosting, boil 3 minutes and then add 1/2 cup chocolate chips. Beat until chips melt. Spread on bars.

Serves 6-8

*Luby's Cafeteria Spaghetti Salad

Ingredients

1 pound spaghetti -- broken in half
16 ounce bottle Italian dressing
1 tablespoon grated Parmesan
cheese
1 tablespoon sesame seeds
1 tablespoon poppy seeds
2 teaspoon seasoned salt
1 teaspoon paprika

1/2 teaspoon garlic powder
1/2 teaspoon black pepper
1/2 teaspoon cayenne pepper
1 medium cucumber -- diced
1 medium red onion -- diced
2 medium tomatoes -- diced
parsley sprigs

1. Cook spaghetti according to package directions. Drain, rinse with cold water, and drain well. Transfer to large bowl.

2. In medium bowl, whisk together Italian dressing, cheese, seeds, seasoned salt, paprika, garlic powder and peppers until well blended.

3. Stir in cucumber and onion.

4. Pour over spaghetti and toss lightly to coat evenly.

5. Cover and refrigerate at least 2 hours or up to 24 hours.

6. Garnish with tomatoes and parsley sprigs.

Serves 12

*Macaroni Grill Chocolate Cake with Fudge Sauce

Ingredients

1 3/4 cups mayonnaise
1 3/4 cups cold brewed coffee
(room temp.)
1 1/2 teaspoons vanilla
3 1/2 cups flour
1 tablespoon baking soda
1 cup cocoa powder

1 1/2 cups granulated sugar
1 cup heavy whipping cream
8 ounces semisweet chocolate, cut
into 1/4 inch pieces

1. Preheat oven to 350 degrees F.

2. Sift flour, baking soda, cocoa powder and sugar.

3. Mix ingredients, but do not over mix. Batter should be thick.

4. Pour batter into a 13 x 9 inch pan.

5. Bake at 350 degrees F for 25 minutes or until toothpick inserted in center comes out clean.

6. To make the fudge sauce, bring cream to a simmer over medium heat in a nonreactive saucepan. Be careful not to burn.

7. Remove from heat and add chocolate.

8. Let sit for 5 minutes.

9. Whisk the glaze smooth.

10. To serve, cut a large square of cake, and place on a plate. Pour warm fudge sauce over cake. Top with a scoop of vanilla ice cream and nuts.

Serves 6-8

*Macaroni Grill Focaccia

Ingredients

9 tablespoons olive oil, divided use
3 cups unsifted all-purpose flour
3/4 cup unsifted semolina flour
1/2 teaspoon salt, divided
1 1/2 tablespoons quick-rising dry yeast
1 1/2 cups hot milk (between 120 to 130 degrees F)
1 tablespoon fresh rosemary leaves

1. Pour a 1/2 tablespoon of the olive oil into a 9-inch square cake pan; spread to cover bottom and sides.

2. Place all-purpose flour, semolina flour, 2 tablespoons of the olive oil, 1/4 teaspoon of the salt and all of the yeast in the bowl of a mixer fitted with a dough hook or you can mix by hand.

3. Mix ingredients on medium speed. Reduce speed to low and slowly add hot milk. Increase the speed to medium and continue mixing for 5 minutes, then knead about 10 minutes by hand.

4. Dust the bottom of cake pan with a little flour. Remove dough from bowl and spread out evenly in pan. Cover with a towel and let it rest for 30 minutes.

RecipeSecrets.net tip: Store in a plastic bag at room temperature, and use within a few days.

5. Preheat oven to 400 degrees F.

6. Remove towel and brush dough with 1 to 2 tablespoons of the olive oil. Dust the top with additional salt and rosemary. Bake for 20 minutes.

7. Remove from oven and drizzle with remaining oil.

Serves 6-8

*Macaroni Grill Reese's Peanut Butter Cake

Ingredients

3/4 cup Unsalted butter
3/4 cup Creamy style peanut butter
2 cups Packed brown sugar
3 Eggs
2 cup Unsifted all purpose flour
1 tablespoon Baking powder
1/2 teaspoon Salt
1 cup Milk
1 teaspoon Vanilla

Peanut Butter Filling:
1 cup Cream cheese, softened
1/2 cup Creamy style peanut butter
Chocolate Glaze:
1/2 cup Water
4 tablespoons Unsalted butter
1/2 cup Cocoa
1 cup Unsifted powdered sugar
1 teaspoon Vanilla

1. Preheat oven to 350 degrees F. Grease and flour two 9" cake pans.

2. In a large bowl, cream butter and peanut butter until it becomes fluffy. Mix in brown sugar. Add eggs, one at a time, mixing after each addition.

3. In a small bowl, combine flour, baking powder and salt. Add flour mixture to butter mixture with milk and blend. Add vanilla.

4. Pour batter into pans. Bake until cake tests done, about 45 minutes. Cool on wire rack to room temperature before frosting the cake.

5. Spread 3/4 cup peanut butter filling over tops of each cake. Let chill.

6. Spread half of warm Chocolate Glaze over peanut butter topping on each cake, using metal spatula dipped in hot water. The glaze will cool as it thickens.

Peanut Butter Filling: Cream ingredients together until fluffy.

Chocolate Glaze: Place water and butter in small saucepan. Bring to boil. Add cocoa, sugar and vanilla to water mixture. Mix until smooth.

Makes 2 Cakes

*McCormick Montreal Steak Seasoning

Ingredients

4 tablespoons salt
1 tablespoon black pepper
1 tablespoon dehydrated onion
1/2 tablespoon dehydrated garlic
1/2 tablespoon crushed red pepper
1/2 tablespoon dried thyme
1/2 tablespoon dried rosemary
1/2 tablespoon dried fennel

1. Mix together and store in a shaker.
2. Shake or rub 1 tablespoon seasoning onto steaks.

Serves 1

RecipeSecrets.net tip:
This seasoning goes well on beef, chicken, pork and more !

*Olive Garden Angel Hair and Three Onion Soup

Ingredients

1/2 pound pearl onions
1 medium red onion sliced thin
1 medium Vidalia onion sliced thin
4 tablespoons olive oil
6 cups chicken stock
Salt
1/4 teaspoon Red Pepper flakes

1/2 pound Angel Hair,
   broken in 2 inch pieces
1/4 cup chopped Italian Parsley
4 teaspoon grated Romano Cheese

1. Place onion and oil in a large sauce pan over low heat and saute, stirring occasionally, about 20 minutes, until onions are soft.
2. Add stock and salt to taste. Sprinkle with hot pepper flakes and simmer for about 1 hour.
3. Add pasta and parsley and cook until pasta is al dente. Sprinkle with grated Romano cheese.

Serves 6

America's Most Wanted Recipes: Volume 2

*Olive Garden Beef Filets In Balsamic Sauce

Ingredients

6 beef tenderloin filets (6 oz size)
4 tablespoons extra virgin olive oil
4 tablespoons butter
1 yellow onion, medium and sliced thin
1 pinch salt
1 pinch black pepper
1/2 cup dry white wine
1/2 cup marsala wine

1/2 cup beef broth
2 tablespoons balsamic vinegar
1 dash parsley, finely chopped
6 fresh rosemary sprigs

1. Heat oil and butter in a large saute pan over medium heat. Add sliced onions, salt, and pepper; cook 10 minutes or until softened and browned.

2. Add both wines, broth, vinegar and bring to a boil. Reduce heat and simmer for 10-15 minutes or until sauce is reduced by half.

3. Rub filets with oil; season with salt and pepper.

4. Grill filets to desired doneness.

5. Arrange onions and sauce on a platter and top with steaks. Garnish with parsley and sprigs of rosemary.

Serves 6

90

*Olive Garden Chicken Crostina

Ingredients

6 boneless, skinless chicken breasts
2 cups & 1 tablespoon flour
1 tablespoon salt
1 tablespoon pepper
1 tablespoon Italian seasoning
1 tablespoon roasted garlic, minced
1 cup white wine
1 ½ cups heavy cream
5 tablespoons olive oil
1 pound linguine
1 cup parmesan cheese, grated

1 cup roma tomatoes, cored & diced
2 tablespoons parsley, chopped
Potato Crust
1 ½ cup seasoned breadcrumbs
¼ cup parmesan cheese, grated
¼ cup melted butter
½ teaspoon garlic powder
¼ cup parsley, chopped
1 small potato, peeled & grated
Salt & pepper to taste

1. Mix all ingredients for Potato Crust in a bowl and set aside.

2. Mix 1 ½ cups flour, salt, pepper and Italian seasoning in a shallow dish. Dredge chicken in the mixture, shaking off any excess.

3. Heat 3 tablespoons oil in a large skillet. Cook chicken breasts 2 at a time over medium-high heat until golden brown and crisp, or until internal temperature reaches 165 degrees F. Add more oil for each batch as necessary.

4. Place cooked chicken breasts on a baking sheet or dish and top with potato crust mixture. Transfer baking sheet to a pre-heated broiler until golden brown (1-2 minutes).

5. Cook pasta according to package directions. Drain and set aside.

6. Heat 2 tablespoons oil in a sauce pan. Add roasted garlic, cook for 1 minute. Stir in 1 tablespoon of flour and wine and bring to a boil. Add cream, parmesan cheese, 1 tablespoon parsley, and tomatoes. Sauce is done when it is bubbling throughout and begins to thicken.

7. Coat pasta with sauce, then top with chicken and remaining sauce. Garnish with chopped parsley

Serves 6

*Olive Garden Chicken San Marco

They say, "When you're here, you're family", but sometimes a family meal is best spent at home. This recipe uses Wondra flour. Wondra flour is a quick mixing flour. It dissolves instantly even in cold liquids. It's perfect for lump free sauces and gravies.

Ingredients

1 cup green bell pepper, julienne
1 cup red bell pepper, julienne
1 3/4 cups broccoli florets, cut small
1 cup zucchini, slice 1/4" then halve
1 cup yellow squash, slice 1/4" then halve
3 Tbs pure olive oil
Pasta:
6 cups fresh fettuccine; cook, drain
1 tablespoon pure olive oil
San Marco Sauce
3 tablespoon pure olive oil
2 pounds chicken thigh meat (skin-less/boneless, cut in 1" cubes)

2 large yellow onions, 1/8" dice
1 cup carrots; peel, julienne
1 tablespoon garlic, chop fine
1 cup chicken broth
1 can Italian plum tomatoes, (28 oz) w/juice
1 teaspoon dry oregano
1 teaspoon dry rosemary
3/4 teaspoon salt
1/2 teaspoon black pepper
2 teaspoon Wondra flour

1. Preheat a heavy non-aluminum 6-qt pot over medium-high heat and add the olive oil.

2. Once oil is hot, add the chicken pieces and saute for 5 minutes until lightly browned on all sides.

3. Add the onions and carrots and saute, about 2 minutes.

4. Add the garlic and saute about 30 seconds. Do not burn the garlic.

5. Then add the chicken broth to the pot. Stir to loosen bits and pieces from the pan.

6. Add all additional ingredients including the flour, lower the heat to a simmer. Cover and simmer, stirring occasionally, until the chicken pieces are tender, about 5 to 10 minutes.

7. While the sauce is finishing cooking, add 3 Tbs oil to a skillet and saute the bell peppers, squash and broccoli over medium heat until just tender and crisp.

8. Add the vegetables to the sauce when the chicken is cooked, mix together

9. Add salt, pepper and herbs, to taste.

10. Toss the cooked pasta with 1 Tbs oil to prevent sticking and add to the sauce; mix chicken, vegetables and sauce and serve along with Parmesan cheese.

Serves 6

*Olive Garden Chocolate Lasagna

Ingredients

Cake
6 cups cake flour, sifted
5 1/4 cups granulated sugar
2 1/4 cups Hershey's Cocoa
2 tablespoons baking soda
4 1/2 cups milk
1 1/2 cups butter
12 large eggs
1 tablespoon vanilla extract

Butter Cream
2/3 cup water
4 tablespoons meringue powder
12 cup sifted confectioners' sugar
1 1/4 cups shortening
3/4 teaspoon salt
1 teaspoon clear almond extract
1 teaspoon clear vanilla extract
1 teaspoon colorless butter flavor

1. Heat oven to 350 degrees F. Grease three 10-inch springform pans.
2. In mixing bowl, combine sifted flour, sugar, Cocoa & baking soda.
3. Add butter and mix well.
4. Add milk, eggs and vanilla and mix. Pour about 5 cups of the cake batter into each pan.
6. Bake 45 minutes or until toothpick inserted in cake center comes out clean.
7. Cool for 10 minutes before you remove the cake from the pan. Transfer to a wire rack to cool.
8. To make the butter cream, combine water and meringue powder; whip at high speed until peaks form. Add 4 cups of sugar, one cup at a time, beating after each addition at low speed.

9. Add shortening and remainder of sugar. Add salt, extracts and flavorings; beat at low speed until smooth. Thin out 1/2 of the frosting with a little water. The thinned frosting is used as the filling between layers.

10. Place one 10 inch cake on a large round cake platter. Spread 1/2 of the thinned frosting on top. Sprinkle with semi-sweet chocolate chips. Place the second cake on top of the first. Frost the top with the remaining thinned frosting. Sprinkle with semi-sweet chocolate chips. Place the third layer on top of the second. Frost the top with all of the Butter Cream that was not thinned. Sprinkle with semi-sweet chocolate chips.

Makes 1 Cake

*Olive Garden Fettuccine Assortito

Ingredients

1 cup Green bell pepper, julienne
1 cup red bell pepper, julienne
1 3/4 cups broccoli flowerets, cut small
1 cup zucchini, sliced 1/4" thick
1 cup yellow squash, sliced 1/4" thick
1 cup carrots, cut into matchsticks
1 3/4 cups ham, julienne
1 pound fettuccine, cooked al dente
3 cups Fontina cheese sauce

3 tablespoons butter or margarine
3 tablespoons olive oil

Fontina Cheese Sauce
6 tablespoons butter
6 tablespoons all-purpose flour
3 cups milk
6 ounces fontina cheese, shredded
salt and pepper

1. To make the sauce, use a heavy non-aluminum pot and melt butter. Add all-purpose flour and cook on moderate heat for 2 minutes, while stirring with a wire whisk.

2. Add milk and bring just to the boil. Turn off the heat and add Fontina cheese and mix into the hot milk. Adjust the salt and pepper.

3. For the pasta, add the butter and olive oil to a large skillet over medium heat and saute the vegetables and ham together until slightly tender. Stir frequently.

4. Drain the pasta and toss with the vegetable & ham mixture; add the hot sauce and toss again to coat all ingredients with the sauce.

Serves 4-6

*Olive Garden Five Cheese Lasagna

Ingredients

4 cups Mozzarella cheese, shredded
1 cup Lasagna noodles, spinach or egg
Marinara sauce, as desired
Parmesan cheese, freshly grated

Cream Sauce:
1/4 cup Butter
1/4 cup Flour
2 cups Milk

Cheese Filling:
1/4 cup Sun-dried tomatoes, oil packed,
  minced
1 tablespoon Fresh garlic, minced
3 1/2 cups Ricotta cheese
3 Eggs
1 cup Grated Parmesan cheese
1/4 cup fontina cheese
1/2 cup Grated Romano cheese
1/2 teaspoon Salt
1 teaspoon Black pepper

1. To make sauce, melt butter over medium heat in heavy, 1 quart saucepan.
2. Add flour and stir until blended, about 1-2 minutes.
3. Add milk, stirring with wire whisk as it comes to a simmer. Cook and stir until thickened (3-4 minutes). Set aside and cool.
4. Drain and minced tomatoes and garlic. Place other cheese filling ingredients in 3-quart mixing bowl with tomatoes and garlic.
5. Add 1-1/2 cups of cooled cream sauce and mix well. Refrigerate, reserving 1/2-cup for later use.
6. Cook lasagna noodles according to the package directions. Drain and run under cold water.
7. Place 3 lasagna noodles in a 9x13x2 lightly oiled baking

dish, overlapping slightly. Spread 1-1/2 cups cheese filling over noodles; sprinkle with one cup mozzarella and 1/4-cup fontina cheese. Repeat pasta and cheese layering three more times; top with remaining three lasagna noodles. Spread 1/2-cup of reserved cream sauce over top and cover with foil.

8. Preheat oven to 350 degrees F and bake covered for 1 hour.

9. Remove from oven and let it sit for 15 minutes before serving. Serve topped with hot marinara sauce and Parmesan cheese.

Serves 2

*Olive Garden Fried Mozzarella

Ingredients

16 oz Package of Mozzarella Cheese
2 Eggs Beaten
1/4 Cup Water
1 1/2 Cup Italian Bread Crumbs
1/2 teaspoon Garlic Salt
1 teaspoon Italian Seasonings
2/3 Cup Flour
1/3 Cup Corn Starch

1. Cut the mozzarella into either triangles or sticks.
2. Beat the eggs with water and set aside.
3. Mix the bread crumbs, garlic salt, and Italian seasonings and set aside.
4. Blend the flour with corn starch and set aside.
5. Heat your vegetable oil for deep frying to 360 degrees.
6. Dip cheese in flour then in egg wash and then coat with bread crumbs.
7. Place carefully in hot oil and fry until golden, this takes just a few seconds so watch carefully.
8. When golden remove from hot oil and drain .

Serve with marinara sauce.

Serves 4

*Olive Garden Lemon Cream Cake

They say when life gives you lemons, make lemonade. Well, why not make lemon cream cake?

Ingredients

1 3/4 cups cake flour
1 tablespoon baking powder
1 teaspoon salt
1/2 cup white sugar
1/2 cup vegetable oil
6 egg yolks
3/4 cup water
1 tablespoon lemon zest
6 egg whites

1/2 teaspoon cream of tartar
3/4 cup white sugar
1 cup heavy whipping cream
2 1/2 cups lemon pie filling
8 slices lemon

1. Preheat oven to 350 degrees F.

2. In a large bowl, combine flour, baking powder, salt, and 1/2 cup sugar.

3. Add oil, egg yolks, water and lemon rind. Beat with an electric mixer until smooth.

4. In a small bowl, beat egg whites and cream of tartar until peaks form. Slowly add 3/4 cup sugar, and beat until stiff peaks form.

5. Fold 1/3 of the whites into the batter, then quickly fold in remaining whites until no streaks remain.

6. Turn batter into ungreased 10 inch tube pan. Bake at 350 degrees F for 60 minutes or until a toothpick inserted in the center comes out clean.

7. Invert cake and cool completely in pan. When cool, loosen edges to remove cake from the pan.

8. To make filling, beat cream to stiff peaks. Fold in lemon filling. Chill until stiff.

9. To assemble cake: Slice cake horizontally into 3 equal layers. Fill layers with 1/3 cup of filling. Spread remaining filling on top layer. Decorate with lemon slices.

Makes 1 cake

*Olive Garden Tuscan Tea

Ingredients

4 ounces Olive Garden Italian Signature Lemon Flavor Syrup
16 ounces Freshly-brewed iced tea

Lemon Flavored Syrup
1 cup water
1 cup sugar
lemon juice, to taste

1. Mix lemon syrup with iced tea. Serve over ice. Garnish with lemon wedge.

RecipeSecrets.net tip:
Substitute other fruit juices to make all kinds of syrups.

Mix this syrup with your favorite alcohol for a great adult beverage.

Lemon Flavored Syrup

1. Heat in saucepan until sugar is dissolved; remove from heat; add lemon juice to taste.

2. Store in covered jar in refrigerator. Use for flavoring iced tea. Mix with water to make lemonade.

Serves 1

*Olive Garden Zuppa Toscana Soup

Ingredients

1/4 cup of olive oil
1 bunch of kale
1 1/2 cup diced onions
1 20 ounce pkg of Hot Turkey
6 cloves of garlic minced
Italian Sausage, casings removed
1/3 cup shredded carrots

5-14 ounce cans chicken broth
2 pounds new red potatoes
 sliced 1/4 " thick with skins
2 cups of water
3 baking potatoes peeled
1/2 to 1 teaspoon red pepper flakes
1/3 cup of half and half

1. Brown the sausage in a skillet with some oil and set aside.

2. In the same pot put 1/4 cup of olive oil and add the carrots and saute for 2 minutes then add the onion and garlic and cook until soft over medium heat.

3. Peel the potatoes and cut into 1 in. cubes and add to the pot with the chicken broth and water. Cook over medium - low heat until the potatoes are tender.

4. Remove the potatoes from the pot and place in a blender with a bit of the broth. Do not over fill and cover and blend until smooth. Return puree to the broth. Salt and pepper to taste.

5. Remove the tough stem from the kale and slice into thin ribbons. Add the kale to the red potatoes and the sausage to the broth. Simmer covered until the potatoes are tender about 10 or 15 minutes.

6. Add any additional salt or pepper to taste, if needed. Add the half and half and heat for a few minutes.

Serves 4

*Outback Steakhouse Cyclone Pasta

Ingredients

1 cup sun-dried tomatoes
1 cup shiitake mushrooms
1 onion
1 (16 ounce) jar alfredo sauce
1 cup chicken breasts, chopped
1 cup of shredded ham
1 (16 ounce) box penne pasta, cooked

Swiss cheese
Italian bread, to serve with
oregano, to taste
thyme, to taste
garlic, to taste

1. Preheat your oven to 375 degrees F.
2. Combine all ingredients in a lightly greased 13 x 9 inch baking dish.
3. Bake for 20-30 minutes or it begins to brown.

Serves 4

*Outback Steakhouse Walkabout Soup

Ingredients

2 1/2 cups chopped sweet onions
1/4 cup butter
3 tablespoons flour
1 1/2 teaspoon salt
1/4 teaspoon pepper
1/2 teaspoon paprika
3 cups milk
1/3 cup cream

2 cups vegetable stock

1 cup shredded cheddar cheese
1/4 cup shredded Mozzarella cheese
1 scallion, chopped

RecipeSecrets.net tip:
Make your own chicken, beef or vegetable stock at home and freeze it for future use.

1. Melt butter in large sauce pan over medium heat.

2. Add onion, and saute for 10 minutes or until tender.

3. Remove from heat and stir in flour, paprika, salt, and pepper.

4. Slowly add milk stirring until smooth.

5. Add vegetable stock, a third at a time, stir until blended.

6. Place over low heat, stirring until creamy, thickened & hot.

7. Add cheddar cheese & cream & stir to melt cheese.

8. Pour into bowls & sprinkle scallions & Mozzarella on top.

Serves 4

*Panera Bread Asian Sesame Chicken Salad

Ingredients

Salad:
2 Wonton wrappers
Canola oil, for frying
2 tablespoons sliced almonds
4 cups romaine lettuce, torn into
bite-sized pieces, loosely packed
1 tablespoon fresh cilantro, chopped
3 ounces boneless, skinless chicken
breast, grilled and sliced thinly

1 tablespoon sesame seeds
Asian Sesame Dressing:
1/4 cup rice wine vinegar
1/4 cup toasted sesame oil
2 tablespoons soy sauce
1 teaspoon toasted sesame seeds
1 teaspoon crushed red pepper flakes
3/4 cup canola or vegetable oil

1. Preheat, the oven to 350 degrees F.
2. Cut the wonton wrappers into 1/4-inch strips.
3. Heat about 2 inches of canola oil to 365 degrees F in a heavy skillet.
4. Fry wonton strips in oil until they are crisp, about 30 seconds. Remove with slotted spoon and drain on paper towel.
5. Spread the almonds out on a sheet pan. Toast them in the oven for 5 minutes, toss them around and then toast for 5 more minutes. Remove and let cool.
6. To make the dressing; in a bowl, mix together all of the ingredients except for the oil. Use a wire whisk to blend well and then slowly drizzle in the oil to create an emulsion.
7. In another bowl, toss the lettuce, cilantro, fried wonton strips, chicken and dressing.
8. Transfer to plates and top with sesame seeds and almonds.

Serves 4

*Panera Bread Broccoli Cheese Soup

Ingredients

1 tablespoon butter, melted
1/2 medium onion, chopped
1/4 cup flour
1/4 cup melted butter
2 cups half-and-half
2 cups chicken stock
1/2 pound fresh broccoli
1 cup carrots, julienne

1/4 teaspoon nutmeg
salt & pepper, to taste
8 ounces grated sharp cheddar

1. Saute onion in butter. Set aside.

2. Cook melted butter and flour using a whisk over medium heat for about 4 minutes. Be sure to stir frequently.

3. Slowly add the half-and-half, continue stirring. Add the chicken stock whisking all the time. Simmer for 20 minutes.

4. Add the broccoli, carrots and onions. Cook over low heat until the veggies are tender, about 20 minutes.

5. Add salt and pepper.

6. By now the soup should be thickened. Pour in batches into blender and puree.

7. Return the puree to the pot and place over low heat, add the grated cheese; stir until well blended. Stir in the nutmeg.

Serves 4

*Pat's King of Steaks Philadelphia Cheese Steak

Ingredients

24 ounces thin sliced rib eye steaks or roll steaks
6 tablespoons soya oil
Cheese Whiz
4 crusty Italian rolls
1 large Spanish onion
green and red sweet peppers
mushrooms, sauteed in oil

1. Heat an iron skillet or a non stick pan over medium heat.
2. Add 3 table spoons of oil to the pan and saute the onions to desired doneness remove the onions.
3. Add the remaining oil and saute the slices of meat quickly on both sides. Melt the cheez Whiz in a double boiler or in the microwave.
4. Place 6 ounces of the meat into the rolls. Add onions, and pour the Cheez Whiz over top.
5. Garnish with hot or fried sweet peppers, mushrooms, ketchup.

Serves 4

*Pepperidge Farm Sausalito Cookies

Ingredients

1 pound butter, softened
2 eggs
2 teaspoons vanilla
1 1/2 cups granulated sugar
1 1/2 cups brown sugar
1 teaspoon baking powder
1 1/2 teaspoons baking soda
1 teaspoon salt

5 cups flour
1 1/2 (12 ounce.) packages semi-sweet chocolate chips
3 cups chopped macadamia nuts

1. Cream butter, eggs, and vanilla together in bowl.
2. In a different bowl, sift together the sugars, baking powder, baking soda, salt and flour.
3. Combine the dry mixture with the egg and butter mixture. You may wish to use an electric mixer. Add the chocolate chips and nuts.
4. Shape into 1 inch balls, place 1 inch apart on an ungreased cookie sheet. Bake at 375 degrees F for 10 to 12 minutes.

Serves 8

*Perkins Family Restaurant Pancakes

Ingredients

4 cups Bisquick or Jiffy baking mix
3 extra large eggs, beaten
2 1/2 cups club soda, room temperature
1/4 cup melted vegetable shortening, room temperature

1. Place the dry pancake mix into a large bowl.
2. Add the eggs, club soda and melted shortening. Use a wire whisk to mix until there are no lumps but do not over mix.
3. Preheat your griddle to medium-high heat.
4. Use about 1 tablespoon vegetable oil on the griddle for each pancake; use 1/2 cup batter for each pancake.
5. Flip pancake once when you see open bubbles appear on the surface and the edges look dry around the pancake.

Makes 10 pancakes

*PF Chang`s Szechwan Chicken Chow Fun

Ingredients

4 ounces ground chicken (cooked)
14 ounces chow fun noodles
2 teaspoons minced scallions
1 teaspoon minced garlic
1 teaspoon chili paste
1 teaspoon Szechwan preserved
vegetables (found at Asian market)
2 teaspoons shredded black fungus
mushrooms
1 teaspoon Sesame oil

Sauce:
3 teaspoons soy sauce
2 teaspoons vinegar
2 teaspoons sugar
1 teaspoon oyster sauce
1 teaspoon mushroom soy sauce
2 teaspoons water

1. Heat the wok and add 2 teaspoons of vegetable oil.

2. Stir-fry garlic and chili paste for almost 10 seconds.

3. Add ground chicken and continue to stir fry.

4. Combine all ingredients for the sauce in a bowl.

5. Add black fungus mushrooms and sauce to the chicken and stir-fry for about 10 seconds.

6. Separate the noodles and mix into the wok a little at a time.

7. Continue cooking for 2 to 4 minutes or until the noodles are hot.

8. Mix in sesame oil before serving. Garnish with Szechwan preserved vegetables and minced scallions.

Serves 2

*Pizza Hut Cavatini

Ingredients

1 large green pepper, diced
1 large onion, diced
1/2 stick butter
1 teaspoon garlic powder
1 pound assorted pasta (wheels, shells, spirals, ziti)
1/2 pound pepperoni, sliced thin & cut in half
8 ounces mozzarella cheese (shredded)
1/2 pound hamburger (cooked)
1/2 pound italian sausage (cooked)
1 16 ounce jar meat flavored spaghetti sauce

1. Melt butter over medium high heat in a skillet. Add onions, peppers, and garlic powder. Saute for about 4 minutes.
2. At the same time, cook pasta according to box directions.
3. Heat spaghetti sauce and mix with cooked hamburger and sausage.
4. Grease an 11 X 13 casserole dish. Place 1/2 of the cooked pasta in the dish, followed by 1/2 the vegetables, 1/2 of the pepperoni, and 1/2 sauce. Repeat another layer
5. Spread mozzarella cheese over top.
6. Bake at 350 degrees F for about 45 minutes or until cheese is melted.

Serves 4-6

*Rainforest Cafe Blue Mountain Grilled Chicken Sandwich

Ingredients

4 hamburger buns
4 6 ounce skinless chicken breast
8 slices bacon, cooked
8 slices cheese
4 teaspoons Cajun seasoning
4 tablespoons teriyaki sauce
I cup roasted red pepper
8 whole lettuce leaves

1. Toast hamburger bun.

2. Rub chicken with Cajun seasoning. Grill chicken breast until cooked through.

3. Brush with teriyaki sauce after grilling.

4. Assemble sandwich with lettuce, bacon, cheese and roasted red pepper and serve.

RecipeSecrets.net tip:

This sandwich is served with Safari Sauce.

Get the recipe on the next page.

Serves 4

*Rainforest Cafe Crab Cakes

Ingredients

I pound lump crab meat
1/2 lemon, juiced
I tablespoon Worcestershire sauce
3 egg yolks
1/2 teaspoon dry mustard
1/2 teaspoon black pepper
I pinch red pepper flakes

I pinch Old Bay seasoning
I pinch salt
3 ounces mayonnaise
I cup fresh bread crumbs
1/4 cup fresh parsley, finely chopped
Olive oil for sauteing

RecipeSecrets.net tip:

Use fresh crab meat for the best flavor!

1. Mix together the lemon juice, Worcestershire sauce, egg yolks, mustard, peppers, Old Bay seasoning, salt and mayonnaise in a mixing bowl.

2. Add the bread crumbs and parsley and mix well.

3. Remove any shells from the crab meat if necessary. Add crab meat to the mixture and mix in lightly. Leave some chunks in the crab meat.

4. Make into 3 inch patties and saute in olive oil for 2 to 3 minutes on each side or until brown.

Makes 4

*Rainforest Cafe Safari Sauce

Ingredients

1 (8 ounce) jar mango chutney
1 cup mayonnaise
1/2 cup prepared mustard
1/2 cup honey
2 teaspoons curry powder
Dash hot pepper sauce

RecipeSecrets.net tip:
Try this on your favorite sandwiches or as a sweet & spicy dipping sauce.

1. Spoon chutney into mixing bowl and cut up any large chunks of fruit in the chutney.
2. With wire whisk, blend in mayonnaise. Add mustard, honey, curry powder and hot pepper sauce. Blend until thoroughly combined.
3. Spoon into three 8-ounce jars and seal with lids. Store the sauce and use it on sandwiches.

Makes 3 8-ounce jars

*Red Lobster Caesar Dressing

Ingredients

1/4 cup mayonnaise
1/4 cup bottled Hidden Valley Ranch
1/4 cup Wish bone Italian Dressing
1 tablespoon white vinegar
1 tablespoon water
1 teaspoon anchovy paste

1. Combine all ingredients with wire whisk until perfectly smooth and creamy.
2. Add 1 teaspoon anchovy paste and 2 tablespoon sour cream.
3. Refrigerate dressing tightly covered to use in 30 days.

Serves 2-4

*Red Lobster Cajun Shrimp Linguine

Ingredients

1 pound linguine
2 tablespoon olive oil
2 tablespoon butter
1 chopped white onion, medium
4 cloves finely chopped garlic
1/2 teaspoon dried thyme (crushed)
1/8 to 1/4 teaspoon red pepper flakes
1/8 teaspoon cayenne

1/2 cup chopped fresh flat leaf parsley
Salt and fresh ground black pepper
1 pound shrimp, shelled and deveined,
tails off (21-25)
1/2 cup heavy cream
2 tablespoon tomato paste
Pinch of sugar
Juice of 1/2 lemon

1. Place shrimp in small bowl. Dust with cayenne, salt, pepper and thyme. Toss and let sit.

2. Boil pasta in salted water until al dente. Drain, reserving some of the pasta water.

3. While the pasta is boiling, melt butter in separate pan with olive oil over medium heat.

4. Saute onion until soft, 3 to 4 minutes.

5. Add chopped garlic and red pepper flakes. Stir for 30 seconds and do not let the garlic burn.

6. Add tomato paste, heavy cream and a small pinch of sugar. Stir and continue to cook until blended.

7. Add shrimp and cook 2 minutes.

8. Add pasta and toss, reserved pasta water may be added to moisten if necessary.

9. Allow the shrimp to finish cooking, another 1 to 2 minutes. Do not over cook. Add parsley. Season to taste with additional salt and pepper, if desired. Remove from heat, squeeze 1/2 lemon over and serve.

Serves 4

*Red Lobster Cheese Biscuits

Ingredients

2 cup Bisquick mix
1/2 cup shredded sharp cheddar
2/3 cup milk
1 teaspoon sugar
1/4 cup melted butter
1/4 teaspoon garlic powder

1. Mix Bisquick, cheddar and milk into a soft dough.
2. Beat with a spoon for about 30 seconds.
3. Spoon on to greased cookie sheet. Smooth down tops.
4. Bake for 8 to 10 minutes at 450 degrees F.
5. While baking, mix butter and garlic.
6. Take biscuits from oven when done and brush butter on tops and serve hot.

Serves 4

*Red Lobster Deep-Fried Catfish

Ingredients

4 (8 ounce) catfish fillets
1 cup milk
1/8 teaspoon salt
1/8 teaspoon black pepper
1/8 teaspoon paprika
1 cup cornmeal
vegetable oil

1. Rinse and pat catfish dry.
2. In a shallow dish, mix together milk, salt, pepper, and paprika.
3. Dip pieces of fish in milk mixture. Roll fish in cornmeal and set pieces on waxed paper.
4. Heat almost 2 inches of vegetable oil to 350 degrees F in a heavy skillet.
5. Deep fry fish, turning once, until golden. Drain on paper towels.

Serves 4

*Red Lobster Dungeness Crab Bisque

Ingredients

1 tablespoon minced onion
2 tablespoons butter or margarine
2 tablespoons flour
2 cups chicken broth
2 cups half-and-half
1 pound Alaska dungeness crab meat
Salt, to taste
Chopped parsley

1. Saute onion in butter until soft. Add flour; cook while stirring for 1 minute.
2. Slowly stir in chicken broth and half-and-half; cook 5 minutes while stirring.
3. Break crab into chunks; add to broth.
4. Heat thoroughly and add salt and pepper to taste. Garnish with parsley.

Serves 4

*Red Lobster Fried Chicken Tenders

Ingredients

Marinade
6 medium garlic cloves
2 cups buttermilk
1 1/4 teaspoons ground cumin
1/2 teaspoon salt
1/2 teaspoon pepper
1/4 teaspoon cayenne pepper
4 to 6 boneless, skinless chicken
breasts, cut in strips

Coating
1 1/2 cups unbleached all purpose
flour
1 3/4 teaspoons salt
1 1/2 teaspoons pepper
1/2 teaspoon ground cumin
1 teaspoon cayenne pepper

Safflower oil (for deep frying)

1. Smash and chop garlic. Put garlic in medium bowl.

2. Add buttermilk, cumin, salt, pepper and cayenne and whisk.

3. Place chicken strips in 13 x 9-inch glass baking dish. Pour buttermilk mixture over; turn chicken to coat. Cover and chill overnight, turning occasionally.

4. Place rack over baking sheet. Remove chicken from marinade and set on rack. Drain 10 minutes.

5. Mix flour, salt, pepper, cumin and cayenne pepper in large bowl.

6. Toss chicken strips in batches in flour mixture, turning to coat; shake off excess. Toss each piece again in flour mixture; shake off excess. Transfer chicken to rack on baking sheet. Let stand at least 15 minutes and up to 45 minutes.

7. Line baking sheet with paper towels. Pour oil into heavy large skillet to depth of 3/4 inch. Heat oil over high heat to 375 degrees F.

8. Add chicken strips to skillet. Adjust heat so that temperature remains between 340 and 350 degrees F. Fry until chicken is golden and cooked through, about 10 minutes.

9. Using tongs, transfer chicken to prepared sheet and drain. Transfer chicken to platter and serve.

Serves 4-6

*Red Lobster Hush Puppies

Ingredients

1 cup cornmeal
2 tablespoons baking powder
1/2 teaspoon salt
1/4 teaspoon pepper
1/8 teaspoon white pepper
1/3 cup minced onion
1 large egg, beaten
1/4 cup milk

1. Mix cornmeal with baking powder, salt, pepper, and onion.

2. Mix egg with milk and whisk into cornmeal.

3. Spoon hush puppies into 350 degrees F hot oil and fry until golden brown.

Serves 2

*Red Lobster Trout Vera Cruz

Red Lobster has been allowing you to enjoy the best of the sea for almost 40 years! Why not bring some of that enjoyment home?

Ingredients

2 trout fillets

Marinade
1/4 cup black olives, sliced
1/4 cup green olives, sliced
1/2 cup olive oil
1/2 cup white wine
1 teaspoon oregano

1/2 cup onion, chopped
1/2 cup green bell pepper, chopped
1/2 cup tomatoes, chopped

1. Mix marinade and let sit 10 minutes.
2. Brush the trout with butter, and season with salt and pepper and place in a baking pan.
3. Pour marinade over the fish and bake at 350 degrees F for 20 to 25 minutes.

Serves 2

*Roadhouse Roast Beef and Mashed Potatoes

Ingredients

Garlic Mashed Potatoes:
1 1/3 pounds potatoes
1 cup low fat milk
2 tablespoons butter or margarine
3 garlic cloves -- minced
salt and pepper -- to taste

Roast Beef and Gravy:
10 1/4 ounces beef gravy
1 teaspoon dried thyme
1/8 teaspoon pepper
12 ounces sliced deli roast beef

1. Pierce potatoes with fork; microwave on high about 12 minutes until potatoes are tender.

2. Halve lengthwise; scoop pulp into medium microwave-safe bowl. Mash potatoes with potato masher or beat with electric hand mixer; reserve.

3. Place milk, butter and garlic in small microwave-safe bowl. Microwave on high 2 minutes; thoroughly mix into potato pulp.

4. Mix in additional milk, if necessary, to reach desired consistency.

5. Season with salt and pepper. Microwave on high 1 to 2 minutes until hot.

6. Meanwhile, in 2-quart saucepan combine gravy, thyme and pepper; bring to simmer over medium heat.

7. Add beef slices; heat through. Serve beef and gravy with mashed potatoes.

Serves 2-4

*Ruby Tuesday Shrimp Pasta Parmesan

Ingredients

14-16 large raw shrimp; thawed, shelled and vein removed
2 tablespoons olive oil;divided
4 tablespoons butter;divided
1 teaspoon dried oregano
1 pound cremini mushrooms, sliced (optional)
1 large onion, finely chopped
3 cloves garlic, minced
1 large fresh red tomato, chopped (skin the tomato, half it and squeeze seeds out before chopping.)
1 tablespoon chopped thyme leaves

1/4 teaspoon crushed red pepper flakes
1/2 cup dry white wine
1/3 cup all-purpose flour
4 cups Whole Milk
1 cup heavy whipping cream
1 cup chicken or vegetable broth
1/8 teaspoon fresh ground nutmeg
salt and pepper to taste
1-16 oz box of pasta(Penne, Rigatonni, or Fettuccine)

1. Mix 1 tablespoon olive oil, oregano 1/2 teaspoon salt and fresh pepper. Brush mixture over uncooked shrimp.

2. Preheat grill pan on medium high. Add shrimp and sear about 2 minutes per side or until bright pink. Transfer to a medium bowl.

3. Melt 1 tablespoon butter and olive oil in a saute pan. Add the mushrooms and saute over medium-high heat until the liquid from the mushrooms evaporates.

4. Add the onion, red pepper flakes and thyme, and saute until the onion is clear, about 8 minutes.

5. Add the chopped tomatoes and garlic, saute for 2 minutes then add wine and simmer 2 more minutes or until liquid evaporates. Transfer mushroom-tomato mix-

ture to the cooked shrimp bowl.

6. Melt 3 tablespoons butter in the same pan over medium-low heat. Add the flour, whisk for 2 minutes until blended. Whisk in the milk, cream, broth, nutmeg.

7. Raise the heat to high while stirring to prevent scorching. Reduce heat to low and adjust seasonings. Add salt and fresh pepper to taste. Simmer, uncovered, until the sauce thickens, whisking often, about 15 minutes.

8. Cook pasta until al dente. Toss with sauce. Remove pasta with sauce from stove and add shrimp mixture. Add grated Parmigiano Reggiano and toss before serving.

Serves 4-6

*Ruby Tuesday Super Salad Bar Pasta

Ingredients

3 cups of cooked, boneless skinless chicken
1 10 oz bag of frozen, but thawed broccoli florets
2 cups of diced or shredded deli ham
1 cup of mayonnaise
1 cup of fat free or regular sour cream
1/2 cup of regular or fat free ranch dressing
1 box of Rotini shaped pasta
1 teaspoon pepper
2 teaspoons garlic salt
parsley

1. Cook pasta in a large pot and cook on medium-high for 10 minutes until tender. Drain and cool with running water. Place 1/2 of the pasta in a large dish.

2. Add 1-1/2 cups of chicken onto the pasta and add mayo, 1/2 of the broccoli, 1 cup of ham, along with the ranch dressing. Stir well.

3. Pour the remaining amount of pasta in the dish now and add the remainder of the chicken and ham. Add the sour cream and the remainder of the broccoli. Stir in the garlic salt and pepper.

4. Toss pasta until completely combined.

5. Add parsley for garnish

Serves 8

*Ruth's Chris Steak House Barbecued Shrimp

Ingredients

6 extra large shrimp, uncooked
1/2 stick butter, melted
1 tablespoon hot sauce
2 cloves garlic, chopped
1/4 teaspoon salt
1/2 teaspoon fresh cracked black pepper
1/2 teaspoon finely chopped fresh parsley
dash of dried rosemary
1 lemon

1. Preheat oven to 400 degrees F. Peel and clean the shrimp, leaving the tails on.
2. In an oven safe dish, add the melted butter, hot sauce, garlic, salt, parsley, pepper, and rosemary. Stir until evenly combined.
3. Place the shrimp next to each other in the bottom of the dish and bake for about 8 minutes.
4. Immediately change to broil and cook the shrimp for about 2 minutes more until cooked.
5. Squeeze some fresh lemon juice over the shrimp and serve.

Serves 1-2

*Sara Lee Crumb Cake

Ingredients

2 cup sifted cake flour
2 cup light brown sugar (packed)
1/2 cup margarine
1 egg well beaten
1/2 cup additional flour
2 teaspoon baking powder
1 teaspoon cinnamon
3/4 cup milk

Topping:
1/2 cup brown sugar
1/4 cup sifted all-purpose flour (sift
before measuring)
1/4 cup butter, room temperature
1 teaspoon cinnamon

1. To prepare the crumb topping, use a fork to combine ingredients until crumbly; set aside 1/2 cup of the mixture.

2. To the remaining crumb mixture add remaining ingredients as given above. Beat well with mixer on low speed.

3. Spread evenly in a greased 8-inch square pan. Spread reserved crumbs over top and bake at 350 degrees F for 40 minutes or until inserted toothpick comes out clean.

4. Dust warm cake with powdered sugar before cutting.

Makes 1 cake

*Shoney's Marinated Mushrooms

Ingredients

1 pound fresh, sliced mushrooms
1 pound fresh, whole mushrooms
14 oz. can beef broth
1/2 cup Italian salad dressing
1/2 cup olive oil

1 teaspoon black pepper
2 teaspoons salt

1. Combine all ingredients.
2. Cover with plastic wrap.
3. Place in refrigerator for 24 hours.

Serves 4-6

RecipeSecrets.net tip:

You can replace beef broth with 1/2 cup red wine vinegar.

*Starbucks Black Bottom Cupcakes

Ingredients

Cake Batter:
2/3 cup cocoa
3 cups flour
2 cups sugar
2 teaspoons baking soda
1/2 teaspoon salt
2 cups water
2/3 cup oil
2 tablespoons vinegar
2 teaspoons vanilla

Filling:
8 ounces cream cheese, room temp
1/3 cup sugar
1 large egg
dash salt
1 small bag milk chocolate chips

1. Preheat oven to 350 degrees F.
2. Cream the sugar and cream cheese. Mix in the egg and salt. Now stir in chocolate chips. Set the filling aside.
3. Sift together flour, sugar, cocoa, baking soda, and salt. Next add water, oil, vinegar and vanilla. Mix well.
4. Fill cupcake liners a little more than half full with chocolate batter. Drop about a generous teaspoon of cream cheese mixture on the top of each in the middle.
5. Bake in a 350 degrees F oven for approximately 20 minutes. About 10 minutes into baking, sprinkle some extra chocolate chips on top of each cupcake.

Makes 36 cupcakes

*Starbucks Chocolate Fudge Squares with Mocha Glaze

Ingredients

1/2 cup unsalted butter, at room temp.
1 cup granulated sugar
1 egg
1 cup all-purpose flour
1/4 teaspoon baking powder
2 oz unsweetened chocolate, melted
1/2 cup milk
1 teaspoon vanilla extract
1/2 cup chopped walnuts

Glaze:
1 generous cup powdered sugar
1 tablespoon unsalted butter, at room temperature
1 ounce unsweetened chocolate, melted
1 teaspoon vanilla extract
1/4 cup brewed double-strength coffee, preferably made from dark-roasted beans

1. Preheat oven to 350 degrees F. Butter an 8-inch square baking pan.

2. To make fudge squares: In a large bowl, cream the butter with the sugar and egg.

3. In a small bowl, sift together the flour and baking powder. Add to the butter mixture. Then add the melted chocolate, do not over-beat. Add the milk, vanilla and walnuts, stirring just to blend.

4. Pour the batter into the pan. Bake until the edges begin to pull away from the sides of the pan, about 30 minutes. Allow the cake to cool completely.

5. To make glaze: In a medium bowl, combine the powdered sugar, butter, chocolate and vanilla extract. Stir in the coffee and whisk until smooth.

6. Refrigerate the glaze until cool, then pour over the top of the cake and cut the cake into squares.

Serves 4-6

*Starbucks Gingerbread Loaf

Ingredients

1 1/2 cups all-purpose flour
2 teaspoons ground cinnamon
1 teaspoon ground cloves
2 1/4 teaspoons ginger
1 teaspoon salt
1/2 cup butter, softened
1 cup white sugar
1 teaspoon orange extract, optional

1 cup applesauce
1 teaspoon baking soda

Frotsing
1 (8 oz.) pkg. cream cheese, softened
1 teaspoon vanilla extract
1/2 teaspoon orange extract
2 1/2 cups confectioner's sugar

1. Preheat your oven to 350 degrees F. Grease and flour a loaf pan.

2. In a medium bowl, mix together flour, cinnamon, cloves, ginger, and salt. Then, set aside.

3. In a large bowl, cream butter and sugar until fluffy. Stir in orange extract.

4. Mix baking soda into applesauce and stir into creamed butter mixture. Add flour mixture. Mix until smooth.

5. Pour batter into prepared loaf pan.

6. Bake at 350 degrees F for 40 to 50 minutes or until a toothpick inserted into center of cake comes out clean.

7. To prepare the frosting, beat cream cheese until fluffy. Beat in vanilla and orange extract. Slowly beat in confectioner's sugar.

8. Once the cake has cooled, evenly spread the frosting on top. Decorate with chopped candied orange peel or candied ginger .

Makes 1 Loaf

*Subway Sweet Onion Sauce

Ingredients

1/2 cup light corn syrup
1 tablespoon minced white onion
1 tablespoon red wine vinegar
2 teaspoons white distilled vinegar
1 teaspoon balsamic vinegar
1 teaspoon brown sugar
1 teaspoon buttermilk powder

1/4 teaspoon lemon juice
1/8 teaspoon poppy seeds
1/8 teaspoon salt
pinch cracked black pepper
pinch garlic powder

1. Combine all ingredients in a saucepan.
2. Heat uncovered on medium-high heat for about 2 minutes until mixture comes to a boil.
3. Whisk well, and remove from the heat. Cover and let cool.

Serves 4

RecipeSecrets.net tip:
This tastes great on sandwiches.
Store in the refrigerator for up to a month.

*T.G.I. Friday`s Honey Mustard Dressing

Ingredients

4 tablespoons honey
2 tablespoons mustard
1 tablespoon white vinegar
1/2 cup mayonnaise
1/2 cup sour cream

1. Measure all of the ingredients into a bowl and mix using a wire whisk.
2. Serve immediately or refrigerate.

Serves 2-4

*T.G.I. Friday`s Orange Cream

Ingredients

6 ounces orange juice
2 teaspoon Grenadine
1 scoop vanilla ice cream
1/4 cup crushed ice

Garnish:
pineapple slice
Maraschino cherry

1. Measure all of the ingredients into a blender.
2. Blend at high speed for 1-2 minutes.
3. Serve in a tall glass and garnish with a pineapple slice and cherry.

Serves 1

*T.G.I. Friday's Shrimp Marinara

Ingredients

1 ounce garlic butter
6 shrimp
6 ounces marinara sauce
10 ounces angel hair pasta, cooked
1 teaspoon parsley, chopped
French bread, sliced
1/2 tablespoon garlic butter

1. Heat a saute pan over medium heat.

2. Add garlic butter and heat for 30 seconds.

3. Add shrimp and saute until cooked and shrimp turns pink.

4. Flip the shrimps once and cook another 1-2 minutes.

5. Add marinara sauce and stir to mix ingredients.

6. Place one serving of hot pasta in center of a bowl and top with sauce, distributing shrimp evenly. Garnish with chopped parsley.

7. Toast French bread slices and brush with garlic butter.

Serves 1

*T.G.I. Friday`s Sizzling Chicken and Cheese

Ingredients

2 (4-oz) chicken breasts
2 tablespoons olive oil
1 teaspoon chopped garlic
1/2 cup shredded Chihuahua white cheese
2 slices American cheese
Mashed Potatoes
Marinade:
2 tablespoons chopped garlic
2 tablespoons chopped parsley

2 ounces olive oil
1 teaspoon crushed red chilies
1/4 teaspoon black pepper
1/4 teaspoon salt
Pepper & Onion Medley:
1 green pepper, julienne
1 red pepper, julienne
1 yellow onion, julienne

1. Trim fat and pound chicken breast.

2. Combine all marinade ingredients. Put chicken breasts in marinade and refrigerate for 3 hours.

3. Slice peppers and onions and saute in olive oil for 2 minutes. Then add 1 tsp chopped garlic and continue to saute another 2-3 minutes. Season with salt and pepper.

4. Saute chicken breasts on both sides in olive oil over medium heat.

5. Heat a cast iron skillet over medium heat until very hot then remove from the burner.

6. Place mashed potatoes on the bottom of skillet. Cover with pepper and onion medley then cheese. Add chicken to top of pepper and onion medley.

7. Top with chopped parsley. Serve directly from skillet.

Serves 2

*Taco Bell Beef Chalupa Supreme

Ingredients

I pound ground beef
1/4 cup. flour
I tablespoon chili powder
I teaspoon paprika
I teaspoon salt
I tablespoon dried minced onion
1/2 cup water
flat bread (pita will work)
oil (for deep-frying)

sour cream
shredded lettuce
shredded Cheddar-Jack cheese
diced tomatoes

1. Mix dried onion with water in a small bowl and let sit for five minutes.

2. Combine ground beef, flour, chili powder, paprika and salt. Add onions and water then mix. In a skillet, cook beef mixture. Stir often while cooking to prevent large chunks from forming; it should be like a paste.

3. Remove from heat but keep warm.

4. In a deep-fryer, or a skillet, deep fry the bread for 30 seconds. Let drain on paper towels.

5. Make Chalupas starting with meat, then sour cream, lettuce cheese, and tomatoes in that order. Top with hot sauce or salsa, to taste.

Serves 4-6

*Union Pacific Apple Pancakes

Ingredients

1 cup flour
1/4 teaspoon salt
1 1/2 teaspoon baking powder
1 tablespoon melted butter
1/2 cup milk
1 beaten egg
1/2 teaspoon vanilla
1 1/4 cup homemade applesauce

1. Sift flour, salt and baking powder.
2. Combine butter, milk and egg. Stir into flour.
3. Add vanilla and applesauce. Beat well.
4. Spoon batter into a hot, well greased griddle, allowing enough batter to make 4" cakes. When edges are slightly browned, turn and cook on other side.
5. Serve hot with maple syrup and of butter.

Serves 6

*Union Pacific Grilled White Pekin Duck Breast

Ingredients

4 skinless White Pekin duckling breasts
4 navel oranges
1 tablespoon sesame oil
1 tablespoon soy sauce
2 tablespoons fresh mint, minced
1 tablespoon sugar
1 red onion, sliced into thin rings
1 small bunch green seedless grapes, stemmed

1 head escarole, cored and chopped into 1-inch pieces
6 ounces baby red romaine leaves
1 tablespoon grape seed oil
Salt and freshly ground pepper, to taste

1. Juice three of the oranges.

2. Combine orange juice with the sesame oil, soy sauce, minced mint, sugar and red onion. Mix well, and season with salt and pepper.

3. Marinade the duck breasts in this mixture for about 30 minutes. Remove duck and save the marinade.

4. In a small saucepan, boil leftover marinade for 1 minute. Season if necessary. Let cool

5. Segment the remaining orange by slicing off the top and bottom. Set orange on flat side, carefully cut away skin and all of pith. Then, slide the knife between each membrane to remove just the fruit. Add grapes to oranges, and set aside.

6. Preheat your grill.

7. Pat duck breasts dry, season on both sides with salt and pepper.

8. Place duck breasts on the grill and cook for about 8 minutes for medium. Remove from grill, keep warm.

9. In a large bowl, lightly toss escarole and romaine with half of the reserved marinade-dressing.

10. Divide greens equally among 4 plates.

11. Slice duck breasts on an angle, and place on top of salad. Scatter citrus segments and grapes over each plateful.

12. In a bowl, mix grape seed oil into remaining dressing. Drizzle remaining dressing over the top of each serving.

Serves 4

*Wendy's Jr. Bacon Cheeseburger

Ingredients

1/8 pound ground chuck
1 potato hamburger bun
1 thin tomato slice
2 slices bacon
1 slice American cheese
2 iceberg lettuce leaves
1/2 tablespoon mayonnaise
1/2 tablespoon ketchup

1. Pre-heat an electric griddle to 375 degrees F.
2. Form a 3 1/2-inch square patty with the ground chuck.
3. Toast the bun faces lightly on the griddle, then set aside.
4. Microwave pre-cooked bacon for 30-40 seconds on a paper towel.
5. Spread the mayonnaise and ketchup evenly on the top bun. Then put the lettuce and tomato on top. Put the bacon on top of the tomato, and then the cheese. Microwave for 15 seconds.
6. Cook the burger patty for about 2 minutes. Salt the top of the burger. Flip the burger and cook for 3 more minutes.
7. Place the burger on the prepared bun.

Serves 1

*Wendy's Spicy Chicken Fillet Sandwich

In 1969, at age 37, Dave Thomas quit his job at Arthur Treacher's to start the first Wendy's in Columbus, Ohio. While other hamburger chains at the time were using frozen beef and mass producing food, Dave Thomas developed an innovative way to make fresh, made to order fast food.

Ingredients

7 cups vegetable oil
1/3 cup Red Hot Pepper Sauce
2/3 cup water
1 cup all-purpose flour
2 1/2 teaspoons salt
4 teaspoons cayenne pepper
1 teaspoon coarse ground black pepper
1 teaspoon onion powder

1/2 teaspoon paprika
1/8 teaspoon garlic powder
4 chicken breast fillets
4 plain hamburger buns
8 teaspoons mayonnaise
4 lettuce leaves
4 tomato slices

1. Preheat 7 cups of oil in a deep fryer to 350 degrees F. You could also use a heavy skillet and fry in small batches. For a healthier version, broil the chicken in the oven

2. Mix the pepper sauce and water in a bowl.

3. Combine the flour, salt, cayenne pepper, black pepper, onion powder, paprika and garlic powder in a different bowl.

4. Pound each of the chicken pieces until about 3/8-inch thick. Trim if necessary to help it fit on the bun. For easy cleanup, place the chicken in a zip bag before pounding.

5. Coat each piece with the flour, then roll it in the watered down pepper sauce. Coat the chicken again in the flour mixture and set it aside. Repeat for other fillets.

6. Fry the chicken for 10 minutes or until they are brown and crispy. Remove the chicken to paper towels to drain.

7. Prepare each sandwich by grilling the face of the hamburger buns on a hot fry pan. Spread 2 teaspoons of mayonnaise on each bun.

8. Place a tomato slice on the mayonnaise, then stack lettuce on top of the tomato.

9. On the bottom bun, place one piece of chicken.

10. Assemble and serve warm.

Serves 4

HELPFUL COOKING TIPS

1. Always chill juices or sodas before adding to beverage recipes.

2. Store ground coffee in the refrigerator or freezer to keep it fresh.

3. Seeds and nuts, both shelled and unshelled, keep best and longest when stored in the freezer. Unshelled nuts crack more easily when frozen. Nuts and seeds can be used directly from the freezer.

4. To prevent cheese from sticking to a grater, spray the grater with cooking spray before beginning.

5. Fresh lemon juice will remove onion scent from hands.

6. Instant potatoes are a good stew thickener.

7. Three large stalks of celery, chopped and added to about two cups of beans (navy, brown, pinto, etc.), will make them easier to digest.

8. When cooking vegetables that grow above ground, the rule of thumb is to boil them without a cover.

9. A scoop of sugar added to water when cooking greens helps vegetables retain their fresh color.

10. Never soak vegetables after slicing; they will lose much of their nutritional value.

11. To cut down on odors when cooking cabbage, cauliflower, etc..., add a little vinegar to the cooking water.

12. Perk up soggy lettuce by soaking it in a mixture of lemon juice and cold water.

13. Egg shells can be easily removed from hard-boiled eggs if they are quickly rinsed in cold water after they are boiled.

14. Keep bean sprouts and jicama fresh and crisp up to five days by submerging them in a container of water, then refrigerating them.

15. When trying to reduce your fat intake, buy the leanest cuts you can find. Fat will show up as an opaque white coating or can also run through the meat fibers, as marbling. Stay away from well-marbled cuts of meat.

16. Pound meat lightly with a mallet or rolling pin, pierce with a fork, sprinkle lightly with meat tenderizer, and add marinade. Refrigerate for about 20 minutes, and you'll have tender meat.

17. Marinating is easy if you use a plastic bag. The meat stays in the marinade and it's easy to turn and rearrange.

18. It's easier to thinly slice meat if it's partially frozen.

19. Tomatoes added to roasts will help to naturally tenderize them.

20. Cut meats across the grain; they will be easier to eat and have a better appearance.

21. When frying meat, sprinkle paprika over it to turn it golden brown.

22. Always thaw all meats in the refrigerator for maximum safety.

23. Refrigerate poultry promptly after purchasing. Keep it in the coldest section of your refrigerator for up to two days. Freeze poultry for longer storage. Never leave poultry at room temperature for more than two hours.

24. If you're microwaving skinned chicken, cover the baking dish with vented clear plastic wrap to keep the chicken moist.

25. Lemon juice rubbed on fish before cooking will enhance the flavor and help maintain a good color.

26. Scaling a fish is easier if vinegar is rubbed on the scales first.

27. Over-ripe bananas can be peeled and frozen in a plastic container until it's time to bake bread or cake.

28. When baking bread, a small dish of water in the oven will help keep the crust from getting too hard or brown.

29. Use shortening to grease pans, as margarine and oil absorb more readily into the dough or batter (especially bread).

30. To make self-rising flour, mix 4 cups flour, 2 teaspoons salt, and 2 tablespoons baking powder, and store in a tightly covered container.

31. Hot water kills yeast. One way to tell the correct temperature is to pour the water over your forearm. If you cannot feel either hot or cold, the temperature is just right.

32. When in doubt, always sift flour before measuring.

33. When baking in a glass pan, reduce the oven temperature by 25 degrees.

34. When baking bread, you get a finer texture if you use milk. Water makes a coarser bread.

35. To make bread crumbs, toast the heels of bread and chop in a blender or food processor.

36. Cracked eggs should not be used as they may contain bacteria.

37. The freshness of eggs can be tested by placing them in a large bowl of cold water ; if they float, do not use them.

38. Dust a bread pan or work surface with flour by filling an empty glass salt shaker with flour.

39. To slice meat into thin strips for stir-fry dishes, partially freeze it so it will be easier to slice.

40. To keep cauliflower white while cooking, add a little milk to the water.

41. A roast with the bone in will cook faster than a boneless roast. The bone carries the heat to the inside more quickly.

42. For a juicier hamburger, add a little cold water to the beef before grilling.

43. To freeze meatballs, place them on a cookie sheet until frozen. Transfer to plastic bags and return to the freezer.

44. When boiling corn, add sugar to the water instead of salt. The salt will toughen the corn.

45. To ripen tomatoes, put them in a brown paper bag in a dark pantry.

46. To keep celery crisp, stand it upright in a pitcher of cold, salted water and refrigerate.

47. When cooking cabbage, place a small tin cup or can half full of vinegar on the stove near the cabbage. It will absorb the odor.

48. Potatoes soaked in salt water for 20 minutes before baking will bake more rapidly.

49. Let raw potatoes stand in cold water for at least a half-hour before frying in order to improve the crispness of French-fried potatoes. Dry potatoes completely before adding to oil.

50. A few drops of lemon juice in the water will whiten boiled potatoes.

51. Buy mushrooms before they "open." When stems and caps are attached firmly, they are fresh.

52. Do not use metal bowls when mixing salads. Use wood or glass.

53. Lettuce keeps better if you store it in the refrigerator without washing it. Keep the leaves dry. Wash the lettuce before using.

54. Never use soda to keep vegetables green. It destroys the Vitamin C.

55. If you over-salt your gravy, stir in some instant mashed potatoes to repair the damage. Add a little more liquid if necessary.

56. After stewing chicken, cool in broth before cutting to add more flavor.

COOKING TERMS

Au gratin: Topped with crumbs and/or cheese and browned in an oven or under a broiler.

Au jus: Served in its own juices.

Baste: To moisten foods during cooking with pan drippings or special sauce in order to add flavor and prevent drying.

Bisque: A thick cream soup.

Blanch: To immerse in rapidly boiling water and allow to cook slightly.

Cream: To soften a fat, like butter, by beating it at room temperature. Butter and sugar are often creamed together.

Crimp: To seal the edges of a two-crust pie either by pinching them at intervals with the fingers or a fork.

Crudites: An assortment of raw vegetables that is served as an hors d'oeuvre.

Degrease: To remove fat from the surface of stews and soups.

Dredge: To coat lightly with flour, cornmeal, breadcrumbs, etc.

Entree: The main course.

Fold: To incorporate a delicate substance into another substance without releasing air bubbles.

Glaze: To cover with a glossy coating, such as a melted and diluted jelly for fruit desserts.

Julienne: To cut vegetables, fruits, or cheeses into match-shaped pieces.

Marinate: To allow food to stand in a liquid in order to tenderize or to add flavor.

Mince: To chop food into very small pieces.

Parboil: To boil until partially cooked; to blanch.

Pare: To remove the outer skin of a fruit or vegetable.

Poach: To cook gently in hot liquid kept just below the boiling point.

Saute: To cook food in a small amount of butter/oil.

Simmer: To cook in liquid just below the boiling point.

Steep: To let food stand in hot liquid in order to extract or enhance the flavor.

Toss: To combine ingredients with a repeated lifting motion.

Whip: To beat rapidly in order to incorporate air and produce expansion.

HERBS & SPICES

Basil: Sweet, warm flavor with an aromatic odor. Use whole or ground. Good with lamb, fish, roasts, stews, ground beef, vegetables, and dressings.

Bay Leaves: Pungent flavor. Use whole leaf but remove before serving. Good in vegetable dishes, seafood, stews and pickles.

Caraway: Spicy taste and aromatic smell. Use in cakes, breads, soups, cheese and sauerkraut.

Chives: Sweet, mild flavor like that of onion. Excellent in salads, fish, soups and potatoes.

Cilantro: Use fresh. Great in salads, salsa, fish, chicken, rice, beans and other Mexican dishes.

Curry Powder: Spices are combines to proper proportions to give a distinct flavor to meat, poultry, fish and vegetables.

Dill: Both seeds and leaves are flavorful. Leaves may be used as a garnish or cooked with fish, soup, dressings, potatoes, and beans. Leaves or the whole plant may be used to flavor pickles.

Fennel: Sweet, hot flavor. Both seeds and leaves are used. Use in small quantities in pies and baked goods. Leaves can be boiled with fish.

Ginger: A pungent root, this aromatic spice is sold fresh, dried, or ground. Use in pickles, preserves, cakes, cookies, and meat dishes.

Marjoram: May be used both dried or green. Use to flavor fish, poultry, omelets, lamb, stew, stuffing and tomato juice.

Mint: Aromatic with a cool flavor. Excellent in beverages, fish, lamb, cheese, soup, peas, carrots and fruit desserts.

Oregano: Strong and aromatic. Use whole or ground in tomato juice, fish, eggs, pizza, chili, poultry, vegetables.

Paprika: A bright red pepper, this spice is used in meat, vegetables and soups or as a garnish for potatoes, salads or eggs.

Parsley: Best when used fresh, but can be used dried. Try in fish, omelets, soup, meat and mixed greens.

Rosemary: Very aromatic. Can be used fresh or dried. Season fish, stuffing, beef, lamb, poultry, onions, and potatoes.

Saffron: Orange-yellow in color, this spice flavors or colors foods. Use in soup, chicken, rice and breads.

Sage: Use fresh or dried. The flowers are sometimes used in salads. May be used in fish, beef, poultry, cheese spreads and breads.

Tarragon: Leaves have a pungent, hot taste. Use to flavor sauces, salads, fish, poultry, tomatoes, eggs, green beans and dressings.

Thyme: Sprinkle leaves on fish or poultry before broiling or baking. Add a few sprigs directly on coals shortly before meat is finished grilling.

ARE YOUR HERBS & SPICES FRESH?

Ingredient Shelf Life:

- Ground Spices 2-3 years
- Whole Spices 3-4 years
- Seasoning Blends 1-2 years
- Herbs 1-3 years
- Extracts 4 years, except pure vanilla, which lasts forever

Still not sure, then use these guidelines:

Check to see that the color of your spices and herbs is vibrant. If the color has faded, chances are so has the flavor.

Rub or crush the spice or herb in your hand. If the aroma is weak and flavor is not apparent, it's time to replace it.

Store herbs and spices in a tightly capped container, and keep away from heat, moisture, and direct sunlight. Replace bottle lids tightly immediately after use.

To minimize moisture and caking, use a dry measuring spoon and avoid sprinkling directly into a steaming pot.

Check the freshness date on the container.

GUIDELINES FOR BUYING FRESH VEGETABLES

Artichokes: Look for compact, tightly closed heads with green, clean-looking leaves. Avoid those with leaves that are brown or separated.

Asparagus: Stalks should be tender and firm; tips should be close and compact. Choose the stalks with very little white; they are more tender. Use asparagus soon after purchasing because it toughens rapidly.

Beans: Those with small seeds inside the pods are best. Avoid beans with dry-looking pods.

Broccoli, Brussels Sprouts, Cauliflower: Flower clusters on broccoli and cauliflower should be tight and close together. Brussels sprouts should be firm and compact. Smudgy, dirty spots may indicate pests or disease.

Cabbage and Head Lettuce: Choose heads that are heavy for their size. Avoid cabbage with worm holes and lettuce with discoloration or soft rot.

Cucumbers: Choose long, slender cucumbers for best quality. Avoid yellow ones.

Mushrooms: Caps should be closed around the stems. Avoid black or brown gills.

Peas and Lima Beans: Select pods that are well-filled but not bulging. Avoid dried, spotted, yellow, or flabby pods.

GUIDELINES FOR BUYING FRESH FRUITS

Bananas: Skin should be free of bruises and black or brown spots. Purchase green and allow them to ripen at home at room temperature.

Berries: Select plump, solid berries with good color. Avoid stained containers which indicate wet or leaky berries. Berries without clinging caps, such as blackberries and raspberries, may be unripe. Strawberries without caps may be overripe.

Melons: In cantaloupes, thick, close netting on the rind indicates best quality. Cantaloupes are ripe when the stem scar is smooth and the space between the netting is yellow or yellow-green. They are best when fully ripe with fruity odor.

Honeydews are ripe when rind has creamy to yellowish color and velvety texture. Immature honeydews are whitish-green.

Ripe watermelons have some yellow color on one side. If melons are white or pale green on one side, they are not ripe.

Oranges, Grapefruit and Lemons: Choose those heavy for their size. Smoother, thinner skins usually indicate more juice. Most skin markings do not affect quality. Oranges with a slight greenish tinge may be just as ripe as fully colored ones. Light or greenish-yellow lemons are more tart than deep yellow ones. Avoid citrus fruits showing withered, sunken or soft areas.

MEASUREMENTS

a pinch	1/8 teaspoon or less
3 teaspoons	1 tablespoon
4 tablespoons	1/4 cup
8 tablespoons	1/2 cup
12 tablespoons	3/4 cup
16 tablespoons	1 cup
2 cups	1 pint
4 cups	1 quart
4 quarts	1 gallon
8 quarts	1 peck
4 pecks	1 bushel
16 ounces	1 pound
32 ounces	1 quart
1 ounce liquid	2 tablespoons
8 ounces liquid	1 cup

Use standard measuring cups and spoons.
All measurements are level.

RECIPES BY CATEGORY

Appetizers

Breakfast

Desserts

Entrees

Salads

TRADEMARKS

- Applebee's is a registered trademark of Applebee's International, Inc.
- Arby's is a registered trademark of Arby's Restaurant Group, Inc.
- Arthur Treacher is a registered trademark of PAT Franchise Systems, Inc.
- Bahama Breeze is a registered trademark of Darden Concepts, Inc.
- Baskin Robbins is a registered trademark of Baskin Robbins.
- Bennigan's is a registered trademark of Metromedia Restaurant Group.
- Boston Market is a registered trademark of Boston Market Corporation which is a wholly owned subsidiary of McDonald's Corporation.
- Bullfush Grill is a registered trademarks of Bullfish Grill.
- California Pizza Kitchen is a registered trademark of California Pizza Kitchen, Inc.
- Carl's Jr is a registered trademark of Carl Karcher Enterprises, Inc.
- Chili's is a registered trademark of Brinker International.
- Church's is a registered trademark of Cajun Operating Company.
- Claim Jumper is registered trademark of Claim Jumper Restaurant LLC
- Cracker Barrel is a registered trademark of CBOCS Properties, Inc.
- Dairy Queen is a registered trademark of International Dairy Queen, Inc. and Berkshire Hathaway Inc.
- Denny's is a registered trademark of DFO, LLC.
- Dollywood is a registered trademark of The Dollywood Company
- El Pollo Loco is a registered trademark of El Pollo Loco, Inc.
- Entenmann's is a registered trademark of George Weston Bakeries, Inc.
- Hard Rock Café is a registered trademark of Hard Rock America, Inc.
- Hardees is a registered trademark of Hardees Food Systems, Inc.
- Hooters is a registered trademark of Hooters of America.
- IHOP and International House of Pancakes are registered trademarks of International House of Pancakes, Inc.
- Ikea is a registered trademark of Inter IKEA Systems B.V.
- Jack In The Box is a registered trademark of Jack In The Box Inc.

- Carinos is a registered trademark of Fired Up Inc.
- Little Debbie is a registered trademark of McKee Foods Corporation.
- KFC, Pizza Hut, Taco Bell, and Long John Silver's are registered trademarks of Yum! Brands, Inc.
- Macaroni Grill is a registered trademark of Brinker International.
- Olive Garden is a registered trademark of Darden Restaurants, Inc.
- Outback Steakhouse is a registered trademark of Outback Steakhouse, Inc.
- Panera Bread is a registered trademark of Panera Bread.
- Pepperidge Farm is a registered trademark of Pepperidge Farm Inc.
- Perkins Family Restaurant is a registered trademark of The Restaurant Company of Minnesota.
- P.F. Chang is a registered trademark of P.F. Chang's China Bistro, Inc.
- Rainforest Cafe is a registered trademark of Landry's Restaurants, Inc.
- Red Lobster is a registered trademark of Darden Restaurants, Inc.
- Roadhouse Grill is a registered trademark of Roadhouse Grill, Inc.
- Ruby Tuesday is a registered trademark of Morrison Restaurants, Inc.
- Sara Lee is a registered trademark of Sara Lee Corporation.
- Shoney's is a registered trademark of Shoney's, Inc.
- Starbucks is a registered trademark of Starbucks Corporation.
- Subway is a registered trademark of Doctor's Associates Inc.
- The Cheesecake Factory is a registered trademark of The Cheesecake Factory, Inc
- T.G.I. Friday's is a registered trademark of T.G.I. Friday's, Inc.
- Wendy's is a registered trademark of Wendy's International, Inc.

To find a restaurant near you, please visit:

Applebee's	http://www.applebees.com
Arby's	http://www.arbys.com
Arthur Treacher's	http://www.arthurtreachers.com
Bahama Breeze	http://www.bahamabreeze.com
Baskin Robbins	http://www.baskinrobbins.com
Bennigan's	http://www.bennigans.com
Boston Market	http://www.bostonmarket.com
Brooklyn Cafe	http://www.brooklyncafe.com
Bullfish Grill	http://www.bullfishgrill.com
California Pizza Kitchen	http://www.cpk.com
Carl's Jr.	http://www.carlsjr.com
Carraba's Italian Grill	http://www.carrabbas.com
Chili's	http://www.chilis.com
Church's	http://www.churchs.com
Claim Jumper	http://www.claimjumper.com
Cracker Barrel	http://www.crackerbarrel.com
Dairy Queen	http://www.dairyqueen.com
Denny's	http://www.dennys.com
Dollywood	http://www.dollywood.com
El Pollo Loco	http://www.elpolloloco.com
Entenmann's	http://www.entenmanns.gwbakeries.com
Hard Rock Cafe	http://www.hardrockcafe.com
Hardee's	http://www.hardees.com
Hooters	http://www.hooters.com
IHOP	http://www.ihop.com
IKEA	http://www.ikea.com
Jack In The Box	http://www.jackinthebox.com
Johnny Carino's	http://www.carinos.com
KFC	http://www.kfc.com
Little Debbie	http://www.littledebbie.com
Luby's Cafeteria	https://www.lubys.com
Macaroni Grill	http://www.macaronigrill.com
McCormick	http://www.mccormick.com
Olive Garden	http://www.olivegarden.com
Outback Steakhouse	http://www.outback.com
Panera Bread	http://www.panerabread.com
Pat's Kind Of Steaks	http://www.patskingofsteaks.com
Pepperidge Farm	http://www.pepperidgefarm.com

Perkins Family Restaurant	http://www.perkinsrestaurants.com
P.F. Chang's	http://www.pfchangs.com
Pizza Hut	http://www.pizzahut.com
Rainforest Cafe	http://www.rainforestcafe.com
Red Lobster	http://www.redlobster.com
Roadhouse Grill	http://www.roadhousegrill.com
Ruby Tuesday	http://www.rubytuesday.com
Ruth's Chris Steakhouse	http://www.ruthschris.com
Sara Lee	http://www.saralee.com
Shoney's	http://www.shoneys.com
Starbucks	http://www.starbucks.com
Subway	http://www.subway.com
Taco Bell	http://www.tacobell.com
The Cheesecake Factory	http://www.thecheesecakefactory.com
T.G.I. Friday's	http://www.fridays.com
Wendy's	http://www.wendys.com

- RECIPE FAVORITES -